Brita
&Eu~~rope~~

Martin Rosenbaum is currently a producer on the *Today* programme on BBC Radio 4. In his previous work for the BBC he was programme editor of *The Week in Westminster,* and made series for Radio 4 on topics such as the nature of British identity and the history of the political interview. Before joining the BBC he worked as a freelance journalist and writer. He is the author of *From Soapbox to Soundbite: Party Political Campaigning in Britain since 1945.* As a freelance he wrote for all the national daily broadsheet papers, most frequently about the media or politics.

Britain &Europe

The Choices We Face

Edited by Martin Rosenbaum

OXFORD

UNIVERSITY PRESS

Great Clarendon Street, Oxford OX2 6DP

Oxford University Press is a department of the University of Oxford.
It furthers the University's objective of excellence in research, scholarship,
and education by publishing worldwide in

Oxford New York

Athens Auckland Bangkok Bogotá Buenos Aires Cape Town
Chennai Dar es Salaam Delhi Florence Hong Kong Istanbul Karachi
Kolkata Kuala Lumpur Madrid Melbourne Mexico City Mumbai
Nairobi Paris São Paulo Shanghai Singapore Taipei Tokyo Toronto Warsaw

and associated companies in Berlin Ibadan

Oxford is a registered trade mark of Oxford University Press
in the UK and in certain other countries

Published in the United States
by Oxford University Press Inc., New York

British Library Cataloguing in Publication Data

Data available

Library of Congress Cataloging in Publication Data

ISBN 0–19–280228–3

1 3 5 7 9 10 8 6 4 2

Typeset by Hope Services (Abingdon) Ltd.
Printed in Great Britain
on acid-free paper by
Cox and Wyman Ltd., Reading

CONTENTS

Acknowledgements   viii
List of contributors   ix

1. Introduction   1

2. The British political context   3
The political battleground   **Andrew Marr**   5
What we think now   **John Curtice**   15

3. The choices for Britain within Europe   21
Britain's future in Europe   **Romano Prodi**   23
Not to use the giant's strength   **Chris Patten**   31
The gamble of engagement   **Timothy Garton Ash**   39

4. The single currency   47
The benefits to business   **Lord Haskins**   49
A threat to the UK economy   **Simon Wolfson**   57
The engine of prosperity   **Lord Layard**   65
The economic costs of membership   **James Forder**   73
The political case for joining
    Dame Pauline Neville-Jones   79
Sovereignty and democracy   **John Redwood**   87

5. Europe and the world   97
The foreign policy challenge   **Lord Owen**   99
Why Europe needs its own defence force   **Charles Grant**   107
The problems for NATO   **Sir Michael Armitage**   115

6. Agriculture and fishing   121
Nonsensicalities and disasters   **Christopher Booker**   123
Why we need the CAP   **Ben Gill**   129

CONTENTS

Improving the policies **Franz Fischler** 137

7. **The environment**   **145**
Common European action **John Gummer** 147
Europe's anti-environmental drift **Stephen Tindale** 155

8. **The social agenda**   **163**
Standing up to the multinationals **John Monks** 165
Red tape kills enterprise **Ruth Lea** 171

9. **Internal democracy**   **179**
The case for a federal Europe **John Pinder** 181
A larger, stronger, more democratic Europe **Tony Blair** 189
Ruled by foreigners **Boris Johnson** 197
Six heretical proposals **Mark Leonard** 203

10. **Culture and identity**   **211**
Britain's cultural place in Europe **Philip Dodd** 213
The diplomacy of the heart **Michael Elliott** 219

11. **The view from the continent**   **227**
Real democracy, not a social science project
Jens-Peter Bonde 229
Becoming a reliable team player **Marta Dassù and
Antonio Missiroli** 237

12. **The view from America**   **245**
How to remain America's privileged partner
Philip Gordon 247
The Atlantic community **Conrad Black** 255

13. **Should we stay or should we go?**   **263**
From the wistful to the inevitable **Nigel Farage** 265
Restating the case **Nick Clegg** 271

14. **Party perspectives**   **279**
Taking the lead in Europe **Keith Vaz** 281
Harmonization or flexibility **William Hague** 287

CONTENTS

An end to vacillation   **Charles Kennedy**   293

Appendix 1: The five economic tests   299
Appendix 2: Member and candidate states   300
Chronology   302
Glossary   305

ACKNOWLEDGEMENTS

Firstly of course my appreciation goes to all the contributors for their articles which form the book.

Within Oxford University Press I am deeply grateful to George Miller for originating the idea, and to him and Rebecca O'Connor for their tremendous efforts in seeing the project through at great speed. Thanks too to Tracy Miller for her meticulous work on the text.

I am also grateful to the prime minister's office for permission to reproduce an extract from his speech in Warsaw in October 2000.

CONTRIBUTORS

Sir Michael Armitage is a former Chief of Defence Intelligence at the Ministry of Defence.

Conrad Black is Chairman and Chief Executive of Hollinger International Inc. and Chairman of the Telegraph Group Ltd.

Tony Blair is Leader of the Labour Party and Prime Minister of the United Kingdom.

Jens-Peter Bonde is a Danish MEP and President of the SOS Democracy intergroup in the European Parliament.

Christopher Booker is a columnist on the *Sunday Telegraph*. His books include *The Castle of Lies — Why Britain Must Get Out of Europe*.

Nick Clegg is Liberal Democrat MEP for the East Midlands and was formerly an official in the European Commission.

John Curtice is Professor of Politics at Strathclyde University and Deputy Director of the Centre for Research into Elections and Social Trends.

Marta Dassù is International Relations Adviser to the Italian Prime Minister, Giuliano Amato.

CONTRIBUTORS

Philip Dodd is Director of the Institute of Contemporary Arts.

Michael Elliott is the editor-in-chief of *eCountries.com* and the former editor of *Newsweek International*. He wrote and presented the BBC series *The Poisoned Chalice* on the history of Britain's relationship with the EU.

Nigel Farage is UK Independence Party MEP for the South East.

Franz Fischler is the European Union Commissioner for Agriculture, Rural Development, and Fisheries, and was formerly the Minister of Agriculture and Forestry in Austria.

James Forder is a Fellow in Economics at Balliol College, Oxford.

Timothy Garton Ash is a Fellow of St Antony's College, Oxford, and of the Hoover Institution, Stanford, and the author of *History of the Present: Essays, Sketches and Despatches from Europe in the 1990s*.

Ben Gill is President of the National Farmers' Union.

Philip Gordon is a Senior Fellow in Foreign Policy Studies at the Brookings Institution in Washington DC, and was formerly Director for European Affairs at the US National Security Council.

Charles Grant is Director of the Centre for European Reform, and was formerly Defence Editor and before that Brussels correspondent of the *Economist*.

John Gummer is a former Conservative Secretary of State for the Environment.

William Hague is Leader of the Conservative Party.

Lord Haskins is Chairman of Northern Foods plc.

Boris Johnson is the editor of the *Spectator*.

Charles Kennedy is Leader of the Liberal Democrats.

Professor Lord Layard is Director of the Centre for Economic Performance at the London School of Economics.

Ruth Lea is Head of Policy Unit, Institute of Directors.

Mark Leonard is Director of the Foreign Policy Centre. His recent publications include *Network Europe*, *The Future Shape of Europe*, and *Making Europe Popular*.

Andrew Marr is Political Editor of the BBC.

Antonio Missiroli is a Senior Research Fellow at the Institute for Security Studies of the Western European Union in Paris.

John Monks is General Secretary of the Trades Union Congress.

Dame Pauline Neville-Jones is a former Political Director and Deputy Under-Secretary of State at the Foreign Office.

Lord Owen is Chairman of New Europe, and was formerly the EU's envoy to former Yugoslavia. He is also a former Foreign Secretary.

CONTRIBUTORS

Chris Patten is the European Union Commissioner for External Relations.

John Pinder is Visiting Professor at the College of Europe, Bruges. His latest book is *The European Union: A Very Short Introduction*.

Romano Prodi is President of the European Commission and was formerly Prime Minister of Italy.

John Redwood is Head of the Conservative Party's Parliamentary Campaigns Unit.

Stephen Tindale is Chief Policy Adviser at Greenpeace UK, and was formerly a special adviser to the Environment Minister Michael Meacher.

Keith Vaz is Minister for Europe.

Simon Wolfson is Managing Director of Next plc.

1 INTRODUCTION

The UK joined the European Economic Community on 1 January 1973. For Edward Heath, the prime minister who took the country in, it was a choice which meant a 'chance for new greatness'. In his view joining meant that 'their Community' would become 'our Community', a Community in which 'we shall be partners, we shall be cooperating, and we shall be trying to find common solutions to common problems'.

The first year of membership, however, demonstrated that Britain's participation in a search for common solutions would not be easy. Food prices went up, while it was revealed that the European Commission was selling surplus butter to the Soviet Union at a cheap, subsidized price; controversy surrounded proposals to allow larger lorries or 'juggernauts' on British roads; plans to achieve economic and monetary union by 1980 were disrupted by the international currency markets; the Community was deeply disunited in its response when war broke out in the Middle East; and Heath found himself isolated in Europe over his demands for a substantial regional fund to channel resources to Britain's deprived areas.

The decision to join was of course the biggest choice, but once Britain belonged it became clear that it was then faced with many difficult choices over the direction of the Community and its role within it. Many of these have echoes today, while other new dilemmas have arisen. This book is about the choices Britain, and the EU, face now. It is a guide to the arguments. The articles in it cover the full range of opinion, from those who want a federal Europe to those who want to withdraw from the EU. And they cover a full range of policy issues—economic, foreign, social, environmental, agricultural, constitutional—as well as underlying themes such as our notions of identity and culture. Each section is intended to make a coherent whole, although inevitably there is some overlap as some topics are raised by writers in more than one section.

As John Curtice shows in his article, the British willingly admit to being comparatively ignorant about the EU. The aim of this book is to allow key participants in the debate over Europe to state their case, so that arguments are clarified, and readers, I hope, will feel themselves better informed.

2 THE BRITISH POLITICAL CONTEXT

THE POLITICAL BATTLEGROUND

Andrew Marr

The first thing is this: whenever two or more British politicians are gathered together talking of 'Europe', they are not talking about Europe. They are not discussing the street life of Paris or Berlin, they are uninterested in the economies of the Mediterranean or the constitutional situation of the German regional governments, they have little knowledge of Polish military concerns or even the Byzantine coilings and uncoilings of the Brussels power game. No, for many years past and to come, in this context 'Europe' means Britain—Britain's future as a self-governing state, Britain's economy, Britain's place in the wider world, Britain's status as a European power, Britain's currency, and even Britain's survivability as a union of different countries.

You can argue that there are other more important things than national destiny, including the world's eco-system, the effect on human life and morality of the latest scientific advances, and world hunger. But for a national politician and for many millions of citizens, the future of the nation matters deeply. It is about mental security, our relationship with our history, a comprehensible democratic system. Hence the intense political emotions roused by the 'European' debate. People who complain about how much air-time and newspaper-space 'Europe' gets are not paying proper attention. It is central. It is about us. Politically, the rest is merely shopping.

The agony of the European question fell first on the shoulders of the Tory party because it was mostly in power during the crucial decades in the second half of the twentieth century. By the late 1950s Harold Macmillan was worried about German domination and French protectionism: 'For the first time since the Napoleonic era, the major continental powers are united in a positive economic grouping, with considerable political aspects, which, though not specifically directed against the UK, may have the effect of both excluding us from European markets and from consultation in European policy.' In other moods Macmillan talked not of Napoleon but of a new Franco-German 'empire of Charlemagne' from which Britain would be excluded. Exclusion: that is the name of the fear that drove nine-tenths of subsequent Tory pro-Europeanism.

A few months after Macmillan had written that, his Lord Chancellor, Lord Kilmuir, warned straightforwardly that signing the Treaty of Rome would lead to a loss of national sovereignty. It meant surrendering some of Parliament's functions to the Council of Ministers; transferring some of the Crown's treaty-making power; and subordinating some of the independence of British courts to the

European Court of Justice. These losses should be frankly admitted, even if doing so made it harder to win the European argument, Kilmuir suggested, or else 'those who are opposed to the whole idea of joining the Community will certainly seize on them with more damaging effect later on'. And so they did: Kilmuir's description of the loss of independent political power, and the perception that people were never really told the truth, has driven nine-tenths of subsequent Tory euroscepticism.

Between those emotional poles, Macmillan's fear of exclusion and Kilmuir's admission of the loss of sovereignty, every dramatic moment of the Conservative argument was played out: the de Gaulle veto on British entry in 1963; the Heath campaign for membership, in 1970–3, including the momentous Commons vote of 28 October 1971, after which Heath celebrated by playing a Bach prelude in Downing Street; Margaret Thatcher's campaign for her money back; her 1988 Bruges speech, restating national sovereignty and taking on 'Brussels socialism'; her loss of chancellor Nigel Lawson and deputy prime minister Geoffrey Howe and subsequent toppling in 1990; the Maastricht dramas under John Major of the early 1990s and Britain's exit from the ERM in 1992 . . . those are the highlights and lowlights of a single consistent and unchanging argument about benefits and pay-offs. The names changed—Common Market, European Economic Community, European Community, European Union—as the political intent grew more explicit. But the hard choice of the trade-off did not essentially change between the first tentative talks about entry and the preparations, now, for a single currency across most of an expanded EU.

On the left of politics, naturally, there were echoes of the Tory argument. Oddly, perhaps, given the old Conservative instinct for Empire, Labour leaders tended to be more emotionally committed to the Commonwealth and suspicious of Europe, from Hugh Gaitskell to Harold Wilson, who produced one of the more memorable early eurosceptic dismissals: 'If there has to be a choice, we are not entitled to sell our friends and kinsmen down the river for a problematical and marginal advantage in selling washing machines in Dusseldorf.' (Which, when we look at the backs of our washing machines today, seems a remarkable piece of over-confidence.) Wilson, of course, moved to being at least vaguely pro-European, allowing his cabinet to campaign on both sides during the 1975 referendum.

But Labour's real change of heart was caused by the voters. First came its crushing defeat as an outright anti-European party, combined with the launch of the pro-European SDP. Then there followed the years in the wilderness where younger Labour politicians like Tony Blair discovered moderate centre-left parties that could win and hold power. Europeanism became a badge of modernity and moderation and, for the New Labour government of today, still is. There is a deep conviction among contemporary Labour politicians that for any party to advocate withdrawal, or seem to be taking Britain on that path, would be electoral suicide. Which takes us back to 2001.

If Blair wins convincingly again this year, he will immediately be faced with an awesomely important and difficult question: should he give the green light, within a year or two, for a referendum on British membership of the single currency? Politically, it would be as great a risk as any taken in peacetime. A 'yes' vote would put Blair where he wants to be, right at the heart of developing a wider, less bureaucratic but undoubtedly still integrationist EU. It would appear to end the argument begun in the 1950s about whether we were really involved — currency is such an intertwining thing, so close to the heart of what sovereignty has always meant. It would, for better or worse, establish Blair finally and unequivocally in British history as a major leader who reshaped the nation's place in the world.

The trouble, of course, is that for a large number of his fellow-citizens it would also end the nation's place in the world, effectively abolishing Britain. To hold and lose such a referendum would seem politically catastrophic, though not all Blair's most senior colleagues agree. He would have been refuted by the people on his major idea and that is a hard thing to recover from, however big your Commons majority. Internally, the five economic tests, at least partly subjective ones, are firmly in the hands of his chancellor, Gordon Brown. Privately, there are at least five or six serious and genuine single currency sceptics in the current Labour cabinet. And public opinion, though fickle, has been long and heavily against such an idea. So the odds are long.

Nevertheless, many Labour insiders believe that a period of serious industrial closures, related to the pound–euro rate, such as dogged the early part of 2001, followed by a continued strengthening of the euro, can shift opinion quite quickly. Blair's problem is that it looks unlikely that he will be able to wait until he knows he can win before declaring the referendum on. A general election win ought not, in economic logic, to have a direct impact. But in terms of public and market expectations it surely will.

Nor is this an issue which is in the sole control of the ruling party. Even if the Conservatives lose the coming general election heavily, their leadership of a Save the Pound movement, with widespread support, has limited Labour's room for manoeuvre. This wider movement, embracing the country's most influential newspapers, well-funded, with passionate backing from many otherwise non-political people, is a force to be reckoned with. But how it will mobilize is still to be decided.

William Hague's critics often fail to ask what would have happened to the Tory party had he not forged a eurosceptic but carefully worded compromise on the currency question in the aftermath of the 1997 defeat. The truth is, his party might have broken in two. He has held it together, however, without losing any significant pro-European figures from the centre-left or any anti-Europeans either. His shadow cabinet contains people judged by their colleagues to be 'outers'—prepared to leave the EU altogether—and his policy of referendums before any further transfer of powers is agreed, plus the renegotiation of already agreed EU deals, is a pugnacious one. But so far a party which was visibly falling apart in office has held together in opposition.

'Outers', however, are a real and under-represented, under-reported group in Britain. Very few mainstream politicians have been prepared to publicly argue that it might be better to leave and, perhaps, seek to join the North American Free Trade Agreement. Looking ahead, though, this coyness is bound to change if a Blair government succeeds, against today's odds, in getting Britain into the euro. Passions are already running high. They will run higher. Any democratic system in which a substantial and angry slice of opinion is virtually unrepresented at national level — the position of the 'outers' in Britain — is taking a risk with itself.

It is impossible, though, to leave this without talking about Europe, in the proper sense of the EU itself. For there are possible ways out of the dilemma that has so trammelled British politics. There is a body of opinion which believes that the EU will and must develop into a formal confederation, with a constitution which limits the powers both of the centre generally and the Commission specifically, ending the old Treaty of Rome dream of 'ever-closer union' in favour of a clear separation of powers between Union, nations, and regions. At the same time, a more open and democratic core would be developed, placing more emphasis on nationally elected leaders and perhaps a new parliamentary chamber drawn direct from national parliaments. This was the vision sketched out in Blair's

Warsaw speech last year and is at the heart of a developing dialogue between Whitehall and Berlin.

Such a looser, wider Europe, open to the Eastern European democracies too, might be easier to sell to a sceptical British public than the more centralized and bureaucratic Europe of the founders. However, as the Nice negotiations showed, this is not universally popular inside the EU. There a grand alliance seemed to be developing between the smaller nations, the current European Parliament, and the Commission, who all have a vested interest in limiting and keeping down a resurgent semi-Gaullist 'Europe des Patries' — an EU forever dominated by Britain, Germany, France, and Italy.

There are many senior politicians at national level and in the Commission who have a different vision — a two-tier Europe with a core group, increasingly integrated in the old way, 'leading the way', surrounded by a skirt or doughnut of nations who want a looser, mainly trading relationship. Although Tony Blair has set his face against that, there are plenty in Britain who would be delighted to have the single market without the single currency or the slew of directives from Brussels. This too is an option which will be increasingly discussed during and after the general election. It is different from, but not necessarily incompatible with, the 'multi-system Europe' envisaged by the Tory foreign affairs spokesman Francis Maude.

'Europe', meaning Britain, has broken prime ministers, splintered parties, destroyed reputations, and mightily bored a large part of the population. It is possible — just — that within the lifetime of the next Parliament a new model will have emerged from the continent which the British can swallow. But any sensible betting person would put money on more broken reputations, resignations, party revolts, and Parliamentary dramas before that happens. Without a settlement of the European dilemma which both allows economic prosperity and the continuation of a meaningful, powerful democracy on these islands, then there will be — can be — should be — no rest.

WHAT WE THINK NOW
John Curtice

Whatever the merits of the arguments for and against further European integration, one thing is clear. The British people are deeply and increasingly sceptical about the EU. On balance we probably just about think that we should remain members of the club. But we know little about it, do not identify with it, and certainly have little interest in becoming more deeply involved. As a result, even if Tony Blair is re-elected to office, he will certainly face an uphill task in persuading us to embrace the euro in any referendum he might hold.

Ever since we voted to stay in the EU in June 1975, the polling company MORI has been asking people in Britain on a regular basis whether they would vote to stay in or to get out of the EU. In the most recent reading, taken in November 2000, slightly more (49 per cent) said they would vote to stay in than said they would opt to get out (44 per cent). But the majority in favour of staying in is a rather fragile one. On two surveys taken in the last two years, those wanting to get out have actually outnumbered those who wanted to stay in

True, as is often the case in survey research, the answers to this issue are sensitive to the terms in which the question is posed. A somewhat differently worded question last asked in the British Election Study immediately after the 1997 general election found that as many as 57 per cent felt that Britain should continue to be a member of the EU while only 28 per cent wanted to 'withdraw'. This contrasts with MORI's reading at the time which, just as it does now, showed only a small majority in favour of 'staying in'. 'Getting out' is evidently a more attractive option than 'withdrawing'. Thus in practice the result of any referendum would probably turn on the relative ability of the two camps to get their position associated with positive language.

Doubtless one reason for this situation is that rather than withdrawing from the EU, the average British voter would probably opt to stay in but make the EU less powerful. For according to the most recent British Social Attitudes survey: only 14 per cent wanted to leave the EU . . . but less than half wanted the EU either to become more powerful (17 per cent) or even just leave things as they are (20 per cent) . . . while as many as 43 per cent wanted to stay in the EU but reduce its powers. Rather than getting out of the Union it appears that what Britain wants is a different kind of EU.

In any event what is undoubtedly true is that Britain is one of the most sceptical members of the EU. Moreover, after having reached a high point of euro-enthusiasm in the early 1990s, the tide of public opinion has been moving against Europe in recent years. According to the latest (spring 2000) wave of the European Commission's own public opinion survey, the Eurobarometer, just 25 per cent of people in Britain now think that their country's membership of the EU has been a 'good thing'. They are almost matched by the proportion (24 per cent) who think it has been a 'bad thing'. Only in Sweden, where 34 per cent consider their country's membership a good thing but equally no less than 38 per cent regard it as bad thing, do people anywhere else in the EU take such a negative view of their country's membership. Across the EU as a whole, those who take a favourable view of their country's membership outnumber those who take a negative view by no less than 35 percentage points.

Meanwhile within Britain answers to this Eurobarometer question have not been as negative as they are now since the early 1980s. Indeed in the early 1990s those thinking our membership was a good thing outnumbered those who thought it was bad by as much as five to one. Equally, when in October 1999 MORI found that a majority wanted to leave the EU, this was the first time they had secured such a reading since 1983. In 1990, in contrast, 62 per cent wanted to stay while just 28 per cent wanted to get out. A similar pattern is also found in the results that have been obtained over the years by the British Election Study and British Social Attitudes surveys.

Our lack of enthusiasm for Europe is matched by our ignorance. The Eurobarometer asked its respondents whether they had heard of each of nine EU institutions. These institutions ranged from the European Parliament (the best known) to the Committee of the Regions (the least well known). The average level of awareness for the nine institutions amongst people in Britain was just 45 per cent, no less than eleven points below that in any other country (Greece). We are well aware of our ignorance too. Asked to give themselves a mark out of ten for how much they thought they knew about the EU, people in Britain on average gave themselves a lower mark (3.5) than did people anywhere else in the EU.

Equally our lack of enthusiasm is matched by a lack of identity. People in Britain simply do not feel European. According to the British Social Attitudes survey, just 17 per cent of us are prepared to call ourselves 'European', whereas no less than 70 per cent of us accept the label 'British'. Similarly according to the Eurobarometer those who feel at all European are outnumbered two to one by those who only feel British. In no other country in Europe is there such a high level of reluctance to acknowledge any kind of European identity.

We also have little trust in EU institutions. Just 27 per cent say that they 'tend to trust' the European Parliament, while 43 per cent tend not to trust it. The equivalent figures for the European Commission are 24 per cent and 40 per cent respectively. Again no other country shows so little faith in either the Parliament or the Commission, which across the EU as a whole are trusted by no less than 52 per cent and 45 per cent respectively.

Little wonder then that Britain also emerges as the country least willing to embrace further European integration. In the most recent Eurobarometer, fewer people wanted the EU to have a more important role in people's daily life in five years' time (just 22 per cent) than was the case anywhere else in Europe.

Meanwhile, according to an ICM survey undertaken at the end of December 2000 and administered in seven other EU countries at the same time, majorities in Britain oppose the creation of a European army, the direct election of the European president, and the harmonization of EU members' legal systems. In contrast, each of these proposals secured clear support in the other seven countries in the survey. And although both this survey and an earlier MORI survey showed a majority were in favour of the creation of the European Rapid Reaction Force, that majority was lower in Britain than it was elsewhere.

Nowhere does this opposition to further integration make itself felt more than on the issue that currently lies at the heart of the debate about Britain's future role in Europe, that is whether Britain should join the single European currency. Not a single survey, whenever taken and however worded, has ever ascertained a majority in favour of joining. Even in the early 1990s when the public was first asked about the idea and, as we have seen, opinion towards Europe in general was relatively favourable, both MORI and the British Election Study found that over half of the public were against joining. More recently support for the idea has been even weaker. Thus in November 2000 both MORI and ICM recorded all-time lows of 22 per cent and 18 per cent respectively in the proportion saying that they wanted to join.

This recent growth in opposition to joining the single currency has probably been occasioned by the early weakness of the euro and the apparent reluctance of Labour ministers to campaign for it. But the fact that opposition to the idea has persisted across a whole decade suggests that it reflects something far more deep-rooted than reaction to short-term developments. As we have seen, few of us feel European. And for many people giving up the pound for the euro means a loss of British sovereignty and identity that they evidently value. In a MORI poll conducted in June 2000, the two most widely cited arguments against joining the euro were 'loss of national identity' and 'loss of sovereignty'. Between them these two reasons were mentioned by no less than 46 per cent of respondents. Meanwhile, when the issue was put to them specifically, no less than 62 per cent agreed that 'joining the euro would mean giving up Britain's national identity'.

Yet despite this deep-seated and growing opposition it still seems that we expect to join the single currency. For example, a MORI survey in January 2001 found that 58 per cent think it likely Britain will have joined by 2010. It seems that in the end we think that a mixture of government persuasion and economic necessity will force us to change our minds. But whether it will be enough to make us more enthusiastic Europeans must remain in severe doubt.

3 THE CHOICES FOR BRITAIN WITHIN EUROPE

BRITAIN'S FUTURE IN EUROPE

Romano Prodi

Britain is a unique and greatly appreciated member of the European family, but her relationship with the 'New Europe' which emerged in the second half of the twentieth century was a troubled one. Tragically late to join, Britain has often seemed an unwilling partner in the creation of the EU. Both Britain and Europe as a whole could have greatly benefited from a more active and enthusiastic British participation in the European project.

Britain has an enormous amount to offer her European partners. The British are famous for pragmatism, common sense, a tradition of administrative excellence, and a long expertise in international relations. The EU also has much to offer Britain. Its single market is the biggest in the world, its environment the best protected, its health and safety standards the highest. Every country which is a member of the EU gains a greater influence in the world than it could ever have alone.

As Tony Blair said in his Warsaw speech in October 2000, Britain's relations with the emerging EU have often been marked by hesitation, alienation, and incomprehension. To fully benefit from and fully contribute to the success of our common project, Britain must put behind it the 'pick and choose' approach of the past. The time has come for Britain to make up its mind about Europe.

I know some people fear that Britain's history, her identity as a nation, will be lost because of the EU. I don't think people should worry on that account. My concern is different: that unless Europe's great nations continue to evolve to keep pace with the rapidly changing world, they will be left behind by the tide of history.

Like Britain, my own country also has a proud history. For centuries, Italy led the world in science, discovery, architecture, medicine, the arts, and culture. Dozens of great Italians left their mark on the history of Europe and the world. But then Italy disappeared from the history books. The days when Italy was a beacon to the rest of Europe came to an end, quite abruptly. Why? The reason was that Europe's other great peoples became nation-states, and Italy missed the boat. The tide of history had moved irresistibly on. Italy's kingdoms and city states simply became powerless over the changing world around them.

It would be tragic if the countries of Europe today made the same mistake, and they in turn disappeared from the history books of future years. I want the twenty-first century to be the century of Europe, not the century when Europe was left behind.

That is not to say that I want Europe to become a continent-sized country—a 'European superstate'—or that I want to strip Britain of its national identity. I don't. I am Italian, and proud of it. I will not give up my national identity. No one is threatening that I should. Nation states are absolutely fundamental to the future of Europe. The EU will not abolish or undermine them. On the contrary, European integration is designed to benefit all our member states, Britain included. In the European system, a great many matters are best left to national governments, if not to regional authorities or town halls.

But the structures of governance which we need to cope with today's global society are new and different. In my view, it is essential to develop new forms of coordination and interaction between the various administrative and political levels, while respecting the principles of proportionality and subsidiarity. What really matters is meeting the needs and satisfying the expectations of our citizens. Europe exists for European citizens, and our efforts today are focused on bringing Europe closer to the people.

At the same time, we have to be aware that many of the problems of the twenty-first century cannot be solved by individual countries acting alone. These issues need to be managed at a European level, where we can achieve more together than any nation could alone. It is to meet these needs that Europe has developed common institutions to find common solutions to shared problems.

In short, a strong Europe needs strong nations—and strong nations need a strong Europe. We should lay to rest the myth that the EU means the abolition of Britain, or Italy, or any of Europe's other countries. If that were true, countries which have recently won their freedom from communism would hardly be so keen to join.

For me, the EU is about three things: peace, strength, and prosperity.

It has always been about peace. Peace was the driving force for the beginning of the European construction. The Second World War remains fresh in the memories of our older citizens to this day. Even the young can remember a Europe divided by the Cold War. Today we have a continent at peace, very soon to be united in democracy as never before. In times of prosperity and comfort it is tempting to take peace for granted. But peace remains the ultimate achievement of the European project, and the ultimate prize for which we are still striving in areas like the Balkans.

The EU is also about strength. Belonging to the EU boosts the influence of every member state. In global trade, for example, the combined negotiating power of the Union gives us far greater clout than any country would possibly have alone. This collective bargaining power ensures the best possible deals for Europe. Strength also means power to influence events. And whether it's a question of protecting the environment, combating cross-border crime, breaking down barriers to business, or reacting to crises on our borders, Europe together is stronger than its many nation-states apart.

Prosperity is the third key reason why we need the EU. Europe means opportunity. Ten years of the single market has proven that. The creation of the single market was a unique achievement—and Britain was a key force behind it. It has helped provide levels of prosperity which past generations could only dream of. Some within the British media often portray the single market as a source of interference, of unnecessary rules and regulations. They forget that the single market removed national boundaries and barriers to trade. These rules are the key to jobs, to wealth, and to new opportunities for British employers and employees alike.

Enlargement will increase these opportunities for business even further. Europe's single market is already the biggest in the world, with 370 million consumers—100 million more than the USA. With the addition of a dozen new countries, it will be unprecedented in human history.

Meanwhile, we are working to make Europe the most competitive economy in the world. The Lisbon summit in March 2000 was a turning point in this respect, with European solutions agreed to tackle the challenges of globalization, the Internet revolution, unemployment, and social exclusion. These are all challenges that require the modernization of our economies. This is another excellent example of what happens when Britain plays a full part.

I could hardly address the question of Britain's future in the EU without touching on the euro. I am regularly asked whether Britain should join. It's not for me to decide. The choice, of course, is for the British people to make. The decision is historic for Britain, as it was for the countries which have already joined, and as it will be for the others who will join in the future.

But I won't pretend that I would wish anything other than for Britain to join. Naturally, I would be delighted to see the UK in the euro. I believe it would be good for Britain, and good for Europe. As an economist, I have always been certain that the single currency will give a powerful stimulus to the European economy, helping business and consumers alike. I remain absolutely confident that its creation will be to the lasting benefit of all its constituent economies. As president of the Commission, I think that for Britain to join our monetary union would be perfectly consistent with other choices made by Britain. It would ensure a greater coherence for the European system as a whole and for Britain's position in Europe.

In conclusion, Europe is entering a profound period of change. Enlargement—perhaps the most significant event in European history since the fall of the Berlin Wall in 1989—will soon take place. It is a truly historic moment for Europe. Twelve or more new countries, most of them recently freed from the communist yoke, will join the Union in the next decade. Europe today is on the verge of being reunited after the Second World War and the Cold War.

I think Winston Churchill would be pleased to see the Iron Curtain not only torn away, but replaced by a democratic association of European nations of both East and West, enjoying freedom to travel, to work, and to do business unhindered by frontiers or barriers. It is a unique achievement in European history, and an inspiring one.

At a time like this, I am amazed that anyone already inside would want their country to leave the EU. But some in Britain still seem to consider themselves new entrants to the club founded by the six original member states of the European Community. Britain has been a member for over 25 years. When 12 or more new countries join, Britain will be one of the oldest members of the club.

I think it is time for Britain to shake off its hesitancy, to feel confident and assured of its place at the heart of Europe. I hope people will see that it is not a question of 'Britain versus Europe'. It never has been. It is Britain and Europe together. We have become, and we will remain, interdependent. Europe needs Britain, and in an age of globalization, Britain needs Europe in order to achieve its own goals of peace, prosperity, strength, and influence in the world. Europe wants Britain to play its rightful role in the Union: a leading role. The British people must decide if they want to assume that role.

NOT TO USE THE GIANT'S STRENGTH

Chris Patten

The story of how Britain missed the boat in Europe in the 1950s has been told many times. Once it became clear that we had no future as a serious European player outside the political and economic construction that was to dominate the second half of the twentieth century it was too late: the institution had already taken shape—and it was an uncomfortable shape for Britain.

But that does not explain the fear and loathing of the EU reflected in much of the British media. This is not a uniquely British phenomenon, of course. The recent Danish referendum was evidence of a wider lack of popular support for the EU, mirrored even in France and Germany. I shall come to that. But the British case is unique. We sometimes come across as a mean-spirited army of 'angry patriots: of the misunderstood and the permanently cross'.

There are many reasons for this. First, as far as Britain is concerned, many people feel they were tricked from the outset. Though the political stakes were clear (Margaret

Thatcher herself spoke at that time of the growing need 'to pool significant areas of sovereignty so as to create more effective political units'), the 1975 referendum was mainly about the commercial benefits expected to flow from Britain's membership of what was usually referred to as the 'Common Market'. There was little focus on Europe's political destiny.

And once it became clear to people that the EU was about more than just trade, no one could agree what it was about. The Treaty evolves continually, and people feel threatened because they can see no natural end-point. Above all, they do not feel they have any control over the process of change through the democratic process.

Secondly, the advent of the EU has accelerated a decline of national parliamentary influence and prestige. This was evident long before the European experiment. When Lord Hailsham warned of an 'elective dictatorship' he was not looking at the European conundrum. But the development of the EU has accelerated the process. There has been an undeniable shift of focus away from Westminster—and this has contributed to public disaffection.

Another source of alienation is that ministers of all governments have treated something called 'Brussels' as an inexorable process quite beyond their control. It has suited their electoral purposes to present the European process not as 'us', but 'them': a continental conspiracy forcing absurd regulations on the British people despite the best efforts of ministers battling on their behalf.

There have also been legitimate doubts about the competence and professionalism of European administration. The EU has much to be proud of as the economic and political focus of Europe's revival in the second half of the twentieth century. It played a major role in the restoration of democracy in Spain, Portugal, and Greece. It is now ready to play a similar role for many countries which had to live for decades in the shadow of the former Soviet Union. But its decision-making process is complex and opaque. As far as the Commission is concerned, there is a major effort underway to reform our processes. I have a particular responsibility for external assistance, and believe we are making real progress there. But it is hard pounding. Multinational bureaucracies in which different cultures must be accommodated are notoriously difficult to run. And people who are prepared to forgive national governments at least some of their shortcomings are less tolerant of the inadequacies of an institution based in another country.

But perhaps the greatest single reason for public alienation has been a lack of emotional commitment in Britain to the EU. The concept of an international society is not one towards which people are attracted by sentiment or tradition. This is a problem not just for the EU, but for all international institutions. The world grows ever more interdependent. We know, intellectually, that nations need to manage their affairs jointly. The problem is how to control and legitimize the organizations created for this purpose. The depth of feeling evident in the muddled movement against globalization shows the fragility of institutions that do not have democratic underpinning.

So how do we move forward? What are our real choices?

Let me dispose, first, of a non-choice. There is no choice to be made between the EU and separate nations in Europe. The concept of the nation-state is alive and well. Indeed it is stronger than ever, and it will be felt ever more strongly as the EU takes in new members in the massive enlargement which is in train. Despite the assiduous and tedious cultivation of the 'superstate' myth, it is no more than that: a bogey invented to frighten the children. The question is not how to protect the nations from the beast, but how the EU and its separate members can best manage their relationship; and how people should be involved, and feel they are involved, in the destiny of the whole.

Nor is there is any choice to be made between Europe and America, as some maintain; or between Europe and the Commonwealth. As Churchill wrote in an essay in 1930: 'from every man will some day be required not the merging or discarding of various loyalties, but their simultaneous reconciliation in a complete and larger synthesis'.

By contrast I believe that Britain does have a choice about her membership of the EU. Some have argued that we would be ruined if we were to withdraw from a market which represents more than 50 per cent of our trade. That is surely wrong. I have no doubt we would be less well off outside than in, but we would survive. The other members of the EU, after all, need our trade as much as we need theirs. The point is not that we would be visited by Biblical plagues, but that we would be diminished as a nation. In international trade we would have to follow World Trade Organization rules shaped by the heavy hitters: the EU and the US. And in our trade with the EU (which would still be most of it) we would have to meet single market rules dictated by our erstwhile partners. We would enjoy all the theoretical sovereignty of staying out by sacrificing the real sovereignty of joining in the decisions that actually shape our lives and our economy. Above all, we would disgrace our heritage by abandoning the leadership of Europe to the great continental powers. That is a choice which Switzerland can make without shame, but it would be wholly at odds with Britain's history.

No, the real choices are otherwise. Let me conclude with two of the most topical.

Should Britain join the euro? The debate is not about the pros and cons of a single currency. It is about whether Britain would be better off inside or outside a project which is happening anyway. There is a serious problem of timing. But I have no doubt that in this as in other areas of policy Britain will lose out if she remains semi-detached as a long-term policy choice. Already the advent of the new currency is having a profound influence on decision-making in Europe. As greater consensus on monetary and even fiscal matters begins to develop in the inner circle of economic policy-making—the so-called eurogroup—I suspect that the economic and competitive arguments for Britain to join, in her own interest, will become very great.

And the same would apply in the international sphere if, for example, the Group of 7 were to begin to give way to a G3, bringing together those with responsibility for the dollar, the yen, and the euro.

How should the EU develop to create greater democratic legitimacy and popular support? This, in my view, is the central question. The most obvious remedy for lack of democratic underpinning would also be the least palatable to those who feel most alienated by the EU: direct election of the European Commission and of its president; and greater authority, including revenue-raising powers, for the European Parliament. The problem with both these approaches is that they would further develop the authority of European institutions at the expense of national ones. The EU has to accept that there is no European 'demos'—in the sense of a population which feels itself to be a single political entity. The European Parliament does a technical legislative job with increasing professionalism, but it is national parliaments (and regional parliaments such as the German Länder) that are, and in my view should remain, Europe's democratic bedrock. At Nice it was agreed that the role of national parliaments should be a central concern in the next stage of institutional development.

One idea now widely canvassed is to create a Second Chamber of the European Parliament especially to consider Europe's overall legislative programme and to apply the principle of subsidiarity: determining which decisions really need to be taken at the European level and which would be better left to the nations. Members could be drawn mainly from national parliaments. In my conception they would not scrutinize all legislation. But they might for example look at proposals that were opposed on subsidiarity grounds by a given number of member states.

If national parliaments are to play the central role I would wish, they need to engage more wholeheartedly in the European enterprise. Westminster, in particular, could do much more. Why not make MEPs ex officio members of the national upper house so that they can help to bind together the national and European policy debates? Parliament should work harder to hold the government to account for positions that ministers take in Europe. In general, there has to be a greater sense that Europe is us, not them. Westminster should begin to take responsibility for European outcomes.

We also need to define more clearly where the boundaries lie between national and Community prerogatives. This, again, was identified at Nice as a central issue for the next stage of institutional development. Tony Blair has spoken of a charter of competences. The Treaty already fulfils that function in a strict legal sense. But people need to be reassured that the EU will exercise restraint in the exercise of its powers ('Oh it is excellent to have a giant's strength, but it is tyrannous to use it like a giant!'—*Measure for Measure*). The issue is complicated because there is often a case for some EU involvement even in areas—such as health, education, culture, and sport, for example—in which the European role should be extremely limited.

Take education. It is generally acknowledged that the Erasmus programme of university exchanges has been an outstanding success. But the EU has no business telling us how to run our schools.

Better demarcation of the respective roles of the EU and of its members might be accompanied by a change in the Treaty confirming that the EU is not, as its opponents like to pretend, an infernal machine ceaselessly accumulating powers at the expense of its members. The founding Treaty calls for an 'ever closer union between the peoples of Europe'. That needs to be balanced by wording to make clear that the EU exists by the will of the member states — and to serve, not to subsume them.

THE GAMBLE OF ENGAGEMENT
Timothy Garton Ash

The choice for Britain in Europe is not what most people think it is. Most people think the choice is whether or not to swap the pound for the euro in order to jump aboard a Franco-German Eurostar train, timetabled from Brussels and heading for Union station. Europhiles say we will thus share sovereignty but gain power and prosperity; europhobes say we will lose sovereignty without gaining either power or prosperity. This picture is ten years out of date — and it was inaccurate even then.

A better metaphor is that of a house. The EU-rope of 15 members is still a house largely designed by French and German architects. We have lived there for more than a quarter-century, as part of a residents' cooperative, and we have had some influence on the interior design. Margaret Thatcher, for example, was instrumental in having a number of rooms knocked together, producing an open-plan arrangement called the single market. But we — meaning the British, but more especially the English — have never been quite comfortable there. We still feel it is really someone else's home. This feeling has been exacerbated by the fact that throughout most of this period the French and German architects, rather ostentatiously proclaiming themselves a 'couple', have repeatedly insisted that nothing important happens without them.

What most people have not noticed is that the house has changed in the last decade, and is about to change even more. In fact, the residents' cooperative has already agreed—at a special meeting in the French seaside resort of Nice—that the house will nearly double in size. Voting cards have been assigned to no less than 12 applicants for membership. Moreover, all the residents now agree that such a large extension—or 'enlargement', as they call it— will mean redesigning and rebuilding the whole house, and changing the way it is run.

Here is a unique opportunity for Britain, one of the weightier and richer residents, to make the place more to our liking. It comes at a time when—as we saw in Nice—the Franco-German couple is not what it was. The German architect is more independent and more powerful than he was before 1990; he feels that he has paid off the debts and moral obligations that he ran up in a disastrous earlier phase of his life; and he is not as committed to his French partner as he used to be. Meanwhile, more recent arrivals such as Spain have grown in strength and self-confidence, while the smaller residents resent being pushed around by the bigger ones. So when it comes to the new design, there are new alliances to be made, and new arguments to be won.

Perhaps this metaphor has become over-extended — as some fear the house itself may do. But it does help to focus attention on the real European choice for Britain, which is whether or not we want to be fully involved in the redesign and building of this new, larger house, over the next 20 years.

No one knows whether and how a community of 27 and more member states can work. Only a dwindling minority in Europe believe that the answer is: as a federal super-state, with its own European government, parliament, and courts. For the direction in which the EU has been developing in recent years is actually away from that. With the notable exception of monetary union — that son-of-Maastricht — the growth areas of community action are mainly inter-governmental: defence and security policy, immigration, and home affairs. If anything, it is the power of the Council of Ministers which has grown relative to that of the Commission.

Yet the question remains: how can this complex, hybrid structure really continue to function without a total blockage caused by the conflicting interests of so many member states? Many would say the Nice summit has already produced a minimalist outcome — and that was with the conflicting interests of just 15 states. At the same time, how can a redesign secure more democratic control? For there is no doubt that there is a crisis of confidence in EU institutions, not just in Britain but right across EU-rope. So the daunting triple task is to make the EU simultaneously larger, more effective, and more democratic.

A number of competing visions have been canvassed—notably by the German foreign minister Joschka Fischer, the French president Jacques Chirac, and the British prime minister Tony Blair in his October 2000 Warsaw speech. The argument will develop over the next three to four years, culminating in a new Inter-Governmental Conference already scheduled for 2004, and linked to the first eastward enlargement, to take in countries such as Hungary, the Czech Republic, and Poland. In short, the formative debate will coincide with what seems likely to be Tony Blair's second term in office.

This debate will be about institutional structures and efficiency. It will be about democracy: does democracy in Europe, as Blair insisted in Warsaw, still primarily derive from the nation-states, and, if so, how can that kind of democratic legitimacy be reinserted into the European project? It will also be an argument between (simplifying greatly) two broad visions of the way Europe should go. One is a Napoleonic vision of an etatist, bureaucratic but also welfare- and social security-providing Europe, a fortress Europe which avowedly aims to become a rival superpower to the US. The other is a liberal, Atlanticist vision of an open, flexible, free-trading Europe, which regards itself a self-confident partner rather than a rival to the US.

My reading of the present European situation is that this argument is up for the winning by the second school, liberal and Atlanticist. Reasons include the movement of opinion in Germany, in the business community, and among the younger generation all over Europe. But the argument can probably only be won decisively for this school if Britain is fully involved in it, as it has been, for example, in the design of the fledgling 'European Security and Defence Identity' and especially the European Rapid Reaction Force. To be sure, American military and political leaders have expressed concern about its 'decoupling' from NATO—but not half as much as they would have done if Britain had not been involved in its design from the outset.

However, can Britain be fully involved in winning that argument, and redesigning the larger house, unless it joins EMU? Increasingly important economic decisions will be made in the Euro-X—currently, Euro-12—group of the members of EMU, rather than in the Economic and Financial Council of the EU. And, rightly or wrongly, both for British and for continental European opinion, EMU membership has become the symbolic test of Britain's European commitment. But the convergence of our economies is not definitely established and EMU, even in its present form, is likely to face great stresses over the next few years.

The real choice for Britain is thus whether to take a historic gamble. The gamble is that, by fully engaging in EU-rope, we can change it into something more like what we think it should be. Only if we were consciously committed to this larger political gamble would it make sense to take the smaller gamble that is membership of EMU.

Some would say that this suggests yet another British illusion about our role and power in Europe. The reason this may not be true, this time, is that there are deeper forces which have already begun changing EU-rope in this direction since the end of the Cold War. On many issues, the scales are finely balanced, and Britain's still significant weight could tip them in the right direction.

There is, in my view, a realistic chance of success. However, one must also countenance two other possibilities. The first is that we fail to persuade our fellow residents to adopt a design of the house with which we can live—and which we feel is better for the house as a whole. The second, which one has to state quite clearly, is that the whole house starts to fall apart, like some 1950s tower block. For—I repeat—no one has ever done this before. There have been smaller groupings of states in European history which have lasted 30, 40, or 50 years. There has never been such a large grouping of European states which has endured for long, and certainly not—as this one must be—on the basis of consent rather than hegemony.

A rational British choice would be based on informed guesswork about the probability of these three different outcomes. This would be a difficult enough exercise at the best of times, but it is made virtually impossible by the extraordinarily distorted and partial picture of Europe which most educated Britons receive from their newspapers, television, and radio—with the newspapers being much the worst. Whatever choice we finally make about the gamble of engagement, one choice we should most certainly make is to start seeing Europe as it really is.

4 THE SINGLE CURRENCY

In 2002 we will see the disappearance of many historic European currencies and the physical appearance of a brand new one—the euro. It will be the culmination of a process of economic and monetary union—at least for the 12 EU countries involved. From 1 January 2002 euro coins and notes will circulate; by 1 July 2002 national currencies will cease to be legal tender.

Europe's economic integrationists have always regarded the fluctuation of exchange rates as inimical to the truly common market they wanted to create. The precursor to EMU was the European Monetary System (EMS), launched in 1979. This included the Exchange Rate Mechanism (ERM), by which those member states involved tried to ensure that their currencies only fluctuated in relation to each other within specified narrow bands. The UK did not join until 1990, and was traumatically forced out by massive speculation in September 1992.

The Maastricht Treaty, signed in 1992, set out the steps towards full economic and monetary union. The participating countries now have fixed exchange rates, financial transactions not requiring physical notes and coins may be made in euros, and interest rates for the eurozone are set by the independent European Central Bank. The final stage, involving the replacement of notes and coins, will take place in 2002. EMU also imposes constraints on the size of public sector deficits, which were laid down under the Growth and Stability Pact agreed in 1997.

The current proclaimed position of the British government is that there is no constitutional bar to being part of the single currency and that it supports the principle of entering, providing it is in the national economic interest to do so. The chancellor of the exchequer, Gordon Brown, has spelt out five rather vague economic tests to be used in making that judgement. If Labour wins the next election and decides to back joining, then it will put the issue to the British public in a referendum—in which case we can all look forward to having to make up our minds on questions like whether the eurozone with Britain added would be an 'optimal currency area'.

For some the question of whether to join is indeed a matter of pragmatic economics, assessing the upside, for example, of exchange rate stability against the downside, for example, of 'one-size-fits-all' interest rates. But for others there are also crucial political issues at stake, involving fundamental questions about democracy or Britain's place and influence in the world.

THE BENEFITS TO BUSINESS

Lord Haskins

My belief is that it would be a significant benefit for the vast majority of British businesses if Britain joined the single European currency, when the right circumstances prevailed. I also believe that the preconditions laid down by the chancellor in 1997 will be satisfied during the course of the next 6–18 months.

Of course some businesses will suffer, because they will find it difficult to cope with a more competitive market, but the successful enterprising ones see the single currency as an opportunity to expand and prosper within the stronger and more effective European single market. Smaller businesses, not directly engaged in external trade, will not see obvious benefits, but will instead have to bear the cost of conversion to the euro. They should be offered financial support by the government to make that conversion.

There are seven substantial benefits to business from a single currency:

- There would be further strengthening of the European single market through the creation of the largest single currency in the world. A key factor in the global competitiveness of US businesses is the scale of their domestic market. Only 10 per cent of US trade is currency related, with 90 per cent of business being transacted in dollars. Britain, outside the euro, has 35 per cent of its trade exposed to currency volatility: inside the euro that figure reduces to 10–15 per cent.
- A single European market, made more transparent and effective because of a single currency, offers consumers more choice and better value, thereby stimulating the market and promoting enterprise.
- Being part of the European currency should bring lower inflation, and lower and more stable interest rates, which will be beneficial to all borrowers, and will stimulate the investment needed to improve Britain's disappointing productivity record.
- The single currency eliminates the costs and time incurred in carrying out transactions between different currency areas.
- Currency volatility, which has been a real problem for most British manufacturers and a catastrophe for British farmers in recent years, would disappear.
- Non-Europeans, keen to trade in the EU, have found Britain a good place to do business, and we attracted about 40 per cent of international investment into the EU during the 1990s. Membership of the single currency will strengthen the attractions of Britain for aspiring outside investors.

- The discipline of sound macroeconomics, arising from participation in the single currency, creates the stable climate which business needs to invest and plan for the medium and long term.

The disadvantages of indefinite exclusion from the euro are self-evident:

- Britain would be increasingly excluded from discussions on macroeconomic strategy in the EU, but as a semi-detached member would still be strongly affected by it.
- Britain could find itself marginalized in the EU, particularly if, as is likely, the two hesitant Scandinavian countries — Denmark and Sweden — eventually decide to commit to the single currency.
- Sterling would continue to be unstable and unpredictable, as it has been for the past 40 years, undermining business confidence and discouraging investment.
- Higher inflation and interest rates are likely to be the price of exclusion, adding a further disincentive to investment.
- The drift of inward investment away from Britain and into Euroland now taking place because of Britain's ambivalence will accelerate if it becomes clear that we will remain outside indefinitely.

Why the eurosceptics and europhobes are wrong

Those businesses who believe that Britain should join the European currency when the conditions are right view with incredulity and alarm the various arguments put forward by the disparate group of opponents of the single currency.

The Conservative Party leader, William Hague, claims that he is in favour of EU membership, but against the euro. But he never has a good word to say for the EU, and indeed has promised to renegotiate many elements of the treaties to which Britain has committed itself over the past 28 years. He knows very well that changes to treaties can only be achieved through unanimity, so the logic of his position is that, when he fails to renegotiate, he has only two options—to withdraw from the EU altogether or to accept the conditions of membership, including participation in the successful single currency. William Hague and Michael Portillo carefully avoid ruling out participation in the euro forever, which suggests that they too recognize that a successful single currency would in the long term be impossible to ignore, however unenthusiastic they might feel about the matter.

Lord Owen also says he is a supporter of the EU, but argues that the single currency is flawed and will be a disaster for all concerned. His group New Europe forecast that the euro would never be launched, because most of the aspiring members would fail to meet the essential monetary preconditions. They were proved wrong and the venture was launched on time in January 1999. They then forecast that the project would collapse very quickly. Again they were wrong. The system is well established and the currency is now expected to strengthen against the dollar and the pound. Now Lord Owen and his colleagues, having been proved wrong twice, argue that even if European Monetary Union proves a success for the 12 or even 14 members, it will never be right for Britain, because of our incompatible economic cycle and greater engagement in dollar trading. This argument is also falling apart, as Britain's economic cycle converges with the EU and moves away from the US, and as its dollar trade, as a percentage of the total, declines and is now not significantly different from that of Germany.

The ultra-nationalist europhobics, such as the Conservative peer Lord Lamont and the Labour peer Lord Shore, have more integrity than the leadership of the Conservative Party, but offer an alternative — complete withdrawal from the EU — which defies credibility and would alarm British businesses if it were considered a serious runner. But it is not. Norman Lamont argues that Norway and Switzerland do very well as small currency areas, so why should not Britain? But their smallness, and their long-time prosperity, due to the peculiar circumstances of oil resources and banking, shelter them from global currency speculators. Britain, with a much larger, more open, and rather less successful economy, has always been at the mercy of the speculators and would continue to be so. Besides, Norway, evenly divided on the issue of the EU, will probably decide to join in the next few years, and some Swiss bankers with a great deal of realism suggest that Switzerland might sign up to the single European currency without necessarily being a member of the EU.

An even more incredible group of critics of the euro suggest that Britain should join the North American Free Trade Area. The idea that she could belong to both is absurd and would be unacceptable to both the EU and NAFTA, so this proposal must lead to withdrawal from the EU. In its place British manufacturers would find themselves 3,000 miles away from their main market in North America. In such an unfair marketplace large sections of British industry would be decimated. Farmers would be wiped out. The experience of Canada's trading relationship with the US is a salutary one. Many Canadian politicians and businesspeople feel overwhelmed by the size of the US economy and by the ruthlessness with which US business has exploited its small neighbour. The Canadian dollar has been steadily depreciating against the US dollar for years. Eurosceptics create scare stories about the dominance of Brussels, but in NAFTA the dominance of the US over the other partners is much greater and much less controllable.

The last group of euro critics belong to the older traditions of the Labour Party, represented by some elements in the trade union movement and people like Arthur Scargill. They argue that the EU is a rich man's club, and ignore the fact that most of its member nations lead the world in their commitment to social justice and workers' rights. They want Britain to maintain the right to devalue and create trade barriers to support the economy. But the quarter-century of steady devaluation and chronic relative under-performance from 1967 to 1992 prove the folly of that approach.

Finally, three economic arguments against Britain joining the euro have to be demolished:

- The first is that national governments, in order to manage their economy, need to maintain control of their interest rates. But as Britain, in line with the US, has recently passed the power to set interest rates from the chancellor of the exchequer to the governor of the Bank of England, the political control of rates has already been abandoned. Furthermore, the idea that a single national interest rate serves the interests of the total national economy is a false one, as Sir Edward George realized when the depressed manufacturing industry of the north-east sought interest rate reductions to suit their needs, but the buoyancy of the south-eastern economy necessitated an interest rate increase. In today's Europe there is not a great deal of difference between the economic performance of the leading countries, but there are huge regional disparities within each of them. London, Paris, Frankfurt, and Milan have much more in common with each other than they have with Newcastle, Lille, Leipzig, and Naples. A common interest rate is essential to a common currency, but it does not and cannot deal with variable regional economic performance.
- The second argument is that a single European currency will only work if there is a single tax system, which in turn would lead to a single European superstate. But any business which trades in the US knows that there is no single federal tax system. Yes, people do pay federal

taxes, but they also pay local and state taxes, which vary enormously. There is no suggestion that the EU aspires to be a US equivalent, but even that federal state is much looser on most issues, except security, than is generally supposed. Employment conditions and the business environment are sharply different between the north-east and the deep south and California. Regions in Europe, as in the US, must be free to set their own tax conditions to suit their local circumstance. Some degree of harmonization, downwards not upwards, may occur in the EU as regions compete with each other to attract investment, but a unitary centralized tax system would be as inappropriate for the EU as it is for the US.

• Finally, there is the risk factor, and of course there are risks in the ambitious single European currency project. There will, as I have suggested, be business losers as well as winners—that is the nature of markets. But enterprising business people know that staying outside the currency is itself risky, and most of us conclude that the benefits of membership far outweigh the risks—and that the risks involved in staying out are much greater than those arising from joining.

A THREAT TO THE UK ECONOMY
Simon Wolfson

Approximately 3,500 years ago Joseph interpreted Pharaoh's dream. He predicted seven years of plenty, followed by seven years of famine. Pharaoh gathered and stored corn during the years of plenty and distributed it during years of famine—a classic policy for managing the cycle. Like so many stories in the Bible there is an uncanny resonance with modern life. The economic cycle of boom followed by recession is still a fact of life. Economies grow, but they grow unevenly.

The story makes two critical points. First, the power of government is required to make an impact on the cycle—without Pharaoh's intervention the market alone would not have prepared for the crisis. Secondly, if Pharaoh had not taken action then his people would have starved. The careful management of the cycle is critical to the economic health of the nation. This essay focuses on why it is essential for the UK to retain control of interest rate policy if it is to effectively manage the cycle.

In a modern economy the most effective way a government and central bank can manage the economic cycle is through interest rates. In a recession interest rates are lowered. This has two positive effects: (i) a reduction in the burden of mortgage repayments increases consumer spending; (ii) a reduction in the cost of borrowing encourages investment in business. So in a recession the lowering of interest rates boosts the economy, thereby lessening the harmful effects of a slowdown. The media attention given to a half-point drop in interest rates is testament to their importance to ordinary people and business alike.

In a boom interest rates should be raised. This slows down the rate of growth, by reducing consumer spending and holding back investment. This action is essential to control inflation and dangerous speculation. If the economy is left unchecked then people and businesses begin to borrow more than they can afford. They rely upon their bonuses to pay off their credit card debts. They depend on house price increases to justify an excessive mortgage. When the bonuses do not come in and house prices fall individuals are left in terrible trouble.

Interest rates are particularly important to the UK economy. Approximately 11 per cent of UK household income is spent on mortgage repayments. This compares with 3 per cent in Germany. Perhaps this accounts for the astonishing speed with which a reduction in rates can affect our economy.

The economies of Europe are very different; there is no magic wand that can make them all the same. There are many profound differences. For example, the UK is a net exporter of oil, Germany a net importer of oil. If the price of oil goes up then the economies will respond in different ways. The fundamental, simple, and unavoidable problem with EMU is that the different economies of Europe move in and out of the cycle at different times and at different speeds.

In order for those economies to be managed effectively they require different movements in interest rates. With one currency, Europe can only have one interest rate — an undisputed fact, a fatal flaw. It is worth examining what happens when interest rates are set at an inappropriate level. How will one interest rate work for two different economies?

Consider this situation: two economies within Europe, one declining into recession whilst the other is booming. What happens to interest rates? Do interest rates go down to help the failing economy or up to control the booming one? Let us assume that the answer is a compromise, that rates are set somewhere between the two extremes. What is the logical consequence? In the booming economy inflation becomes rampant as interest rates are not high enough to slow things down. The economy moves further and further out of control. Personal borrowing becomes unserviceable and asset prices move up so encouraging unrealistic speculation.

This is no longer academic theory. When Ireland joined EMU its rate of inflation was near 2 per cent. Barely two years later inflation is higher than 6 per cent, property prices in Dublin rose by 40 per cent in one year, and personal borrowing is growing at a rate of more than 30 per cent per annum. As yet no one has found a solution to this problem.

In the declining economy interest rates are maintained at too high a rate. Demand remains flat and the people struggle on, locked into a stubborn recession. If this sounds familiar, it should. Remember the ERM? Contrast the fortunes of Ireland with the problems in Germany, where unemployment is still above 9 per cent and recovery is hampered by an interest rate that is still too high. It is little wonder that the majority of Germans do not want to join EMU.

So the booming economy booms more, the slow economy slows down further. The inevitable consequence is that the economies move further out of sync. So as time goes on the compromise interest rate becomes less appropriate for both economies.

Here emerges one of the great paradoxes of EMU. All involved recognize that economies must 'converge' before they can join: yet there has been little or no assessment of the risk of moving apart after joining EMU. So what happens if economies 'diverge' after joining EMU? Logic suggests that if convergence is a prerequisite, any subsequent divergence must be a grave danger. Some people seem to believe that the possession of one currency will lock all economies in sync, but as demonstrated earlier quite the opposite is true. One rate of interest for different economies can only exaggerate the differences. It will come as no surprise that the central issue of divergence is one that is rarely if ever addressed by the proponents of EMU.

If one currency cannot work for the EU how can it work for any country? The simple answer is that there will always be problems with one economic regime for any diverse economy. Even within the UK we have these problems. A dramatic example was the so-called north–south divide in the 1980s. High interest rates appropriate for the booming financial services sector in the south crippled the struggling industrial sector based in the north. The battle against inflation was fought and won, but in the process parts of our economy were lost forever.

In a nation-state the problems, bad as they were, could be mitigated in the following ways:

i   movement of labour out of the depressed areas to areas with good employment prospects — of all the compensating factors this is by far the most important;
ii government borrowing and spending to boost the economy;
iii regional redistribution of wealth through taxation.

As government borrowing is limited by the rules of EMU, I shall deal with movement of labour and taxation.

Mobility of labour is the most effective antidote to regional recession. Every year in the US approximately seven million people cross state borders in order to take up employment. People simply move from the areas of regional decline to the areas that are booming. And this is the crux of the problem with the euro—if you don't speak German, you can't get a job in Germany. The reason the UK is an effective currency area is because we can work anywhere in this country. This is not sentimental nationalism—it is common sense based on a common language. That the boundaries of many economies and states are also the boundaries of language is no coincidence. It is amazing that those who seek to compare the USA to Europe overlook the most obvious and critical difference—the USA has one language, Europe has many. This fundamental difference is of huge economic significance and cannot be ignored. Without a single language there cannot be effective mobility of labour, and without effective mobility of labour there should not be a single interest rate policy.

As for taxation, centrally controlled Europe-wide taxation is not an inevitable consequence of EMU, but the chances of its introduction are very high. The reasons are simple:

i   the regional redistribution of wealth will be the only method left to government to alleviate the effects of localized recession;

ii   there will be central pressure on the booming economies to raise taxes to control inflation (this pressure is already being bought to bear on Ireland);

iii the huge income tax advantages enjoyed by those people living and working in Britain will come to be seen as an unfair advantage.

The clamour for harmonization has already begun. Such measures tend to raise taxes to the highest level; few governments can afford to reduce their tax revenue. However, this argument is not just about the imposition of higher taxes. We should consider the imposition of taxes over which there will be no democratic control. This infringement of our liberty is such an anathema to the British political psyche that one can only assume that people do not really believe that it will happen. If we accept EMU, someday soon our newly elected government will shrug its shoulders and apologize for an interest rate it cannot change, spending it cannot increase, and taxes it does not have the power to reduce.

Ask yourself one final question: why has no one talked to us about what happens if the experiment fails? Perhaps this is the unsinkable ship? That would explain the absence of lifeboats. Ring any bells?

The political and economic risks of joining EMU become more apparent day by day, yet the advantages of joining are unclear and unquantified. The most important reason given for joining is that it will increase trade. I shall now turn to this issue.

The argument runs that the elimination of exchange rate risks will be a huge stimulus to trade. It is my belief that the effect of a fixed exchange rate on trade is vastly over-estimated, particularly where the economies linked by fixed exchange rates have different rates of inflation. Consider the long-term and the short-term risks involved in dealing with a foreign currency. First, most businesses can buy or sell forward, and in this way eliminate the risk of short-term exchange rate fluctuations. This is something that all large importers do. In effect they fix their own rate through the currency markets at minimal cost. Most of our overseas customers will do exactly the same. Second, in the long run fixed exchange rates do not necessarily mean price stability. If inflation is 3 per cent in the UK and 1.5 per cent in Germany then after ten years goods which were the same price will now be much more expensive in the UK. This scenario would make products in the UK unaffordable and cripple exports. The irony is that a floating exchange rate actually compensates for different rates of inflation, and in doing so enhances long-term price stability between nations.

Even if a fixed exchange rate did encourage trade, we need to ask if that benefit would outweigh the cost of losing control of our interest rates. It seems unlikely. How often are individuals seriously affected by the exchange rate? Compare that to the effect we all feel when interest rates are moved. There is no comparison.

In conclusion, EMU makes it impossible to tailor interest rates to the needs of the UK economy. It therefore poses a real threat to the stability of the UK economy. In doing so it threatens the livelihoods of those people who are locked into that economy. The additional cost of this economic instability is a substantial loss of political freedom. EMU is irreversible, and there is no contingency for its failure. The logical and dispassionate arguments are overwhelmingly weighted against joining EMU.

THE ENGINE OF PROSPERITY

Lord Layard

There is only one economic reason to join the euro—that it would give us greater prosperity. To prosper you need to belong to a large market, free of tariffs and non-tariff barriers and undisrupted by currency fluctuations. That is how the USA grew rich. Its huge market enabled firms to specialize and produce on a massive scale at low cost. At the same time the size of the market increased the competitive pressure on firms to be efficient, and widened the range of suppliers from whom consumers could satisfy their needs.

In Europe the Common Market, followed by the single market, has produced some of the same effects. But, as experience has shown, you cannot have a truly single market without a single currency. So the euro is the coping stone of the single market programme which Margaret Thatcher did so much to promote. And it is having its predicted effect. We are now seeing a major reorganization of European industry and finance, to achieve the economies of scale already seen in the USA.

It is easy to underestimate the impact of currencies upon economic life. If (like some monetarists) you believe that money is a veil, it is natural to believe that efficient markets can penetrate the veil. But businessmen know otherwise. If your costs are in sterling and your receipts in a foreign currency whose value fluctuates against sterling, you will be far more cautious about committing yourself to the foreign market.

A good example of how this works comes from Canada, which shares a common frontier and a common language with the USA but not a common currency. Canada trades far less with the USA than geography would lead one to expect. A Canadian province trades one-sixteenth as much with a US state as it does with another Canadian province that is equidistant and of equal income. And because Canada is so weakly integrated into the US market, its productivity is 20 per cent lower than the USA's.

Likewise, Britain's productivity per hour worked is 20 per cent below that on the continent north of the Alps. Among the reasons is our lesser integration into the large European market. That began with our late entry into the Common Market, and it continues with our delayed entry into the euro. After the war European productivity per hour was way behind the US, but the continent has now caught up with the US. Britain, however, lags and has grown no faster than the continent over the last 20 years, despite our economic reforms.

The separate currency is a major reason for this, and it will become even more damaging in the future. Let me explain why.

If you have a separate currency, its value will fluctuate. This creates uncertainty about the return to any long-term investment in export markets. The returns in the foreign currency are already uncertain and, since the currency risk cannot be hedged, this adds further to the uncertainty. On top of this, currencies go through prolonged periods of misalignment, which are deeply damaging even when foreseen. The level of sterling over the last three years has been extremely harmful and is one reason why firms like BMW, Vauxhall, and Corus are rebalancing their businesses away from Britain.

Such misalignments cannot be controlled. For in the modern world of massive short-term capital flows, a floating exchange rate does not serve as a well-balanced adjustment mechanism, as its advocates claim. Experience has shown that a floating exchange rate produces much more variation in competitiveness than occurred in the Bretton Woods period, when the exchange rate could be fixed. As capital becomes ever more mobile through electronically linked financial markets, the exchange rate is likely to fluctuate even more. The simplest remedy is to link ourselves to the currency of our closest trading partners.

The argument would be strong in any case, but it is even stronger when our partners have already linked themselves together. Before that happened, we were in the same position as any one of them. For example, a firm that sold into Germany faced exchange risk whether it produced in Holland, France, Italy, or Britain. Now it faces no exchange risk if it produces in Holland, France, or Italy, but it does if it produces in Britain. So the longer we stay out of the euro, the more firms are likely to move their business to the continent. That is why so many businessmen are urging the government to join the euro—so that they do not have to face that agonizing choice.

The key point is that, once the other countries have linked up, we are no longer in the same situation as before. We cannot choose the status quo ante. If we do not join, we are in a worse situation than before. So, even if we were happy with our previous situation, we cannot avoid a reassessment now that the euro exists.

These are the central economic arguments. But there is another indirect one. Our economy is strongly affected by what happens on the continent—by its level of economic growth and by the regulations we face from Brussels through our membership of the EU. We want to be able to influence these. We can only influence growth in Europe by belonging to the European Central Bank, which sets interest rates on the continent. And we can better influence European regulations if we belong to the committee of the Euro 12 (the countries that belong to the euro). Increasingly European business is done within that group, and at present we are excluded.

That is the case in favour: to avoid currency fluctuations, we must adopt the single currency. But that also means accepting the single rate of interest on that currency.

There lies the rub: we lose control over our own interest rates. So, if Britain faced a shock which affected it differently from other countries, it could not use monetary policy to offset it. This is the problem of one size does not fit all, and it is a serious disadvantage.

However, the same problem occurs in the US. If one region is hit by an adverse shock, the Federal Reserve can do little to help. And yet no one has proposed having separate currencies for different parts of the US. So should Britain be as happy to use the euro as California is to use the dollar?

In this situation Britain's main drawback is that there is much less labour mobility between Britain and the continent than there is between California and the rest of the US. Thus an adverse shock to Britain would be harder to offset by an exodus of population. But there is also of course very low net movement of labour within Britain. Yet no one advocates a separate currency for the north-east of England. Moreover, Britain has one key advantage which California has not—we have the freedom to run a budget deficit. Though in the euro we lose our monetary weapon of stabilization, we still have our fiscal weapon. US states have no such weapon since most of them have to balance their budgets year by year. Thus from the fiscal point of view a European country is better placed than a US state.

The opposite to this is often alleged. It is said that California is better off than Britain would be because, when California's economy plunges, it gets an automatic transfer from the federal budget in Washington. By contrast Britain would get no such transfer from Brussels. However, Britain does not need such a transfer because it has the automatic stabilizers within its own budget. They are stronger than those in the US, and Britain can, if it chooses, use discretionary fiscal change on top of this to offset a recession.

There is one other point. The Californian economy is very different from the average of the US economy. It is highly exposed to idiosyncratic shocks which the Federal Reserve will not offset. By contrast, the economy of Britain is more similar to the overall economy of Europe than the typical US state is to the overall economy of the US. So situations where our interests diverge from those of Europe as a whole should be relatively rare.

We must of course join at a time when our economy is at a similar cyclical position point to the European economy—that is, when we would like to have similar interest rates. Sometime in the next two to three years looks ideal. But there are bound to be times thereafter when British and European interests diverge. That is the cost of joining—in return for the greater benefits of currency stability.

Let me end by reviewing some of the less respectable arguments against joining. First, there is the argument that we should join the large American market rather than the large European one. In other words, join the North American Free Trade Area, not the euro. This is absurd. For powerful economic reasons, over half our trade is with the EU and only 16 per cent with the USA. These powerful forces cannot be bucked. Nor would the rules allow us to join NAFTA and remain in the EU.

Then there is the argument that Europe is failing, so we should stay at arm's length. Europe has indeed one serious weakness. France, Spain, Italy, and Germany all have higher unemployment than we do. While some of the variation is due to cyclical differences, an important part is due to dysfunctional benefit systems and rigid wage structures, which need to be changed. But joining the euro does not mean that we have to copy these countries. Within the British single currency area the south-east has one-third the unemployment of the north-east. So the south-east has not imported the unemployment rate of the north-east. Within any single currency area there will always be local variations, but these are no reason to break up the union.

Third comes the argument that the euro would be a rerun of the Exchange Rate Mechanism. The contrary is true. The ERM was an ill-fated attempt to peg a separate currency to other currencies. The euro is a decision to merge the currencies so that exchange rates no longer exist.

Perhaps the most strident argument used against the euro is that it is the thin end of the wedge, on the route to a federal Europe in which we are forced to harmonize taxes and many other institutions where we prefer our own variant. There is in fact no such implication. The euro is a self-contained arrangement concerning currencies. Britain can continue to veto tax harmonization and most other changes we dislike, and this is governed by the treaties we

71

have signed, quite irrespective of whether we belong to the euro or not. However, if we do belong to the inner club of Europe, it will in fact be easier rather than harder for us to resist pressures of the kind we disapprove of.

Finally, there is a common view that, while we would be better off inside, it is so difficult to manage the transition that we should not try. There are of course formidable political difficulties in persuading the British people. But it can be done. In the 1975 Common Market referendum 55 per cent of voters were against membership six months before the referendum, but only 33 per cent were against it on the day. This time the key conditions for success will be strong business support (which requires a reasonable exchange rate) and a popular government (which requires a referendum quite early in a parliament). If these are in place, Britain will join the euro sooner than many people expect.

THE ECONOMIC COSTS OF MEMBERSHIP

James Forder

The economic case against the euro, and against British membership, rests on the fact that joining involves a commitment to bad and unaccountable economic policy. If we have bad economic policy, we will have poor economic outcomes. We should not vote for that. In so far as the advocates of the euro take this on board, they either ignore the substance of the argument by assuming away the problems, or else propose that there is some 'political' benefit which can be expected to outweigh the economic costs of membership. Although it is not the subject of this essay, it seems to me most unlikely that a failed economic experiment, causing unemployment and slow growth, will generate anything but acrimony, resentment, and hostility to integrationist politics. That is why, from the beginning of this debate, I have felt that the economics of the euro should make those who hope for political integration and for Britain to be at the heart of Europe its firmest and most determined opponents. I count myself amongst them.

The policy package offered to us by the advocates of the euro has three significant components.

One, the most straightforward, is that the abolition of the pound will mean we can no longer either have exchange rate changes with respect to the rest of the euro area, nor have a different interest rate set by the Bank of England. This is, in itself, a very dangerous undertaking since it supposes that there is never much in the way of a good reason for having different interest rates, and that view is certainly false.

The experience of the latter part of the 1990s demonstrates the desirability of different interest rates. The British economy has been growing rather fast after the long recovery from the recession of the early 1990s. On the other hand, the economy of most of the EU has been stuck at a high level of unemployment. It is not just appropriate but also important in such a case that British interest rates be higher than continental ones. The circumstances could be different, of course—we could have recession in Britain and a boom in Europe. That would be an equally powerful demonstration of the point. If we are forced, by membership of the monetary union, to have the same interest rates, then policy will be poor in one part of the area or another.

Now it might be said that circumstances could be different between France and Germany too, who, apparently calling for different interest rates, have yet opted for the euro. Indeed they could. In fact, they were in the aftermath of German reunification. That was the time Britain left the exchange rate mechanism, beginning the recovery and success we enjoyed thereafter. The French authorities, in contrast, chose to behave as much as possible as if monetary union had begun, and the result for them was a long period of high unemployment. Whatever the precise political explanation of this, it makes no case that the euro offers good economic prospects.

What do the advocates of the euro say? First, they say that there are benefits from exchange rate stability. One is that international trade is likely to be greater if no currency transactions are required. Another is that the elimination of uncertainty about future exchange rates will promote deeper economic integration, and in particular cross-border investment.

The first of these is undeniable, but the idea that the benefits are large enough to determine the issue is absurd. The second idea—that the euro will eliminate uncertainty—appears powerful, but is in fact nothing more than an illusion. Of course it is true that if everything else remains the same, we are unlikely to be the losers from doing business in a more certain environment. But the point of the argument about the desirability of different interest rates is that other things do not stay the same if we join the euro: we lose the ability to set appropriate interest rates. That, quite clearly, increases uncertainty. Business in Britain will have to operate on the basis that at any point in the future we might find ourselves in recession with high interest rates or in a boom with low ones. It is, therefore, only a pretence that the euro brings, on the whole, greater certainty. Rather, it removes one kind of uncertainty, replacing it with another, more serious one.

The second plank of the euro policy package is the international regulation of fiscal policy. The details of the Growth and Stability Pact were agreed after the Maastricht Treaty, but a requirement of conformity with it now accompanies membership of the euro. It seeks to limit government borrowing and make spending and taxation plans subject to international approval. Again, it is not the subject of this essay to argue the politics of the question, but it is astonishing that the advocates of the euro deny that it raises any issue of sovereignty. It would be more honest, although not at all easy, to acknowledge the obvious, and make the best of arguing for it.

The danger of the stability pact arises again from the fact that there are occasions when it would be desirable to have larger government borrowing than it allows. That is not to say that such circumstances are normal, but merely that it makes no sense to assume they never occur. The case in question, of course, is when there is a period of unusually high unemployment. In those circumstances, government revenues have a tendency to fall, because fewer taxes are paid, and their expenditures to rise, because more benefits are paid. Thus, if a deficit is to be avoided, action would have to be taken to reduce expenditure and raise taxes. That action, it should be noted, in itself worsens unemployment, since there is now less expenditure by both the government and by individuals. So, confronted with recession, the rules of EMU require us to take action to make it worse.

Now there are, as is sometimes pointed out, certain escape routes. One of these is that if output falls by more than 2 per cent, the rules of the pact are suspended in the country in question for that year. This is not nearly as generous as is often made out, since falls of this magnitude are very rare. But anyway the point of proper economic management is to prevent such things. Rules which allow proper management only in the event that the disaster has already occurred are perverse. In any case, the 'concession' lasts only while output is falling. Yet the need for government borrowing is determined by the level of output, not its change. If unemployment rises sharply one year and output falls, the rule is suspended. But what of the next year? Unemployment remains high, but unless it continues to fall—heaping disaster on disaster—the pact is back in full operation, requiring the government to deepen recession by reducing its borrowing.

The second point made in support of the stability pact is that it does not altogether prohibit government borrowing but permits deficits of up to 3 per cent of national income. The advocates of the euro have put a fair bit of effort into constructing theoretical arguments to say that 3 per cent is sufficient. But simple observation says they are wrong. The British recession of the early 1990s resulted in unemployment of almost 3 million and a vast and quite proper increase in government borrowing, taking it well beyond the limits of the stability pact for several years (even allowing for suspension in the event of a 2 per cent fall in output). What that pact would have required is huge further cuts in government expenditure or huge tax increases. How can it be imagined that such action could be achieved without unemployment rising further? And how can it be imagined that that would be good policy?

Finally, there is the third objectionable plank of the euro proposal—the status of the European Central Bank. In Britain, the Bank of England is 'independent'. It sets policy as it thinks best in order to meet a target set by the government. But it is an essential aspect of this arrangement, designed to ensure its democratic acceptability, that the government can change that target when it chooses. In the euro, things are rather different. There is no provision for instructing the European Central Bank as to its target, and Article 107 of the Maastricht Treaty even says that democratically elected governments may not 'seek to influence' the central bank. A greater infringement of democratic principles in the realm of economic policy-making is hard to imagine.

The prospect of the euro is a horrible one from any point of view, but no true integrationist should favour a proposal so damaging to our economic prosperity and destructive of our political fabric.

THE POLITICAL CASE FOR JOINING

Dame Pauline Neville-Jones

When people argue about UK membership of the euro area, they are usually talking about something else: their views of the EU in general (and whether they like what they see) and their preferences as regards Britain's place in the world. I shall try to disentangle the threads in the debate to show why I think that the opponents of UK entry into the eurozone are mistaken and why I think the case for joining is going to get even stronger with time.

What are the sceptics' political objections to UK entry? These can be summarized as follows: the EU is too interventionist, too regulated, too protectionist, insufficiently democratic and accountable, and therefore not an organization to which we want to cede more sovereignty — and especially not that supreme symbol of national sovereignty, the pound sterling. These seem to be absolute judgements made for all time, in that opponents do not seem willing to subject them to any test of future reform or success.

In one area — lack of accountability — the sceptics' objections carry force. But a powerful and simple (though not

unique) remedy lies in the hands of European governments themselves. They need to open up to public
scrutiny the proceedings of the Council of Ministers. No
doubt openness would be inconvenient on occasion (is
this why it does not happen?). It is not acceptable, however, for the main legislative body of the Union to act
exclusively behind closed doors on public business, thus
powerfully reinforcing the widespread notion that an
abstract, undemocratic, and unaccountable entity called
'Brussels' has arrogated all power to itself, to the exclusion
of elected national politicians.

So strong are the objections of some sceptics to the EU
that they go so far as to argue that the UK should move
closer to North America and even join the US-led North
American Free Trade Area, which they see as embodying
their preferred values—an Anglo-Saxon model of non-
interventionist shareholder capitalism and free trade.
Becoming part of the US dollar-dominated area on these
terms would unavoidably involve leaving the EU. A much
larger number of other sceptics, while sharing much of the
same underlying philosophy, do not want to wrench the
UK from its current moorings or espouse a covert departure strategy, but they would nevertheless keep the UK
indefinitely out of one of the central features and related
decision-making machinery of an organization to which
they nevertheless attach sufficient importance to wish to
remain a member.

One solution thus proposes that, 3,000 miles of intervening water notwithstanding, the British people should

change their geopolitical positioning fundamentally. Under it, complete sovereignty would in theory at least be restored to the House of Commons, at the price of departure from the single market into which 60 per cent of British exports are sold. One may wonder at the common sense of this. Given the relative scales of the UK and the US, one might also dispute the likelihood of the UK being able either to stop objectionable decisions of Congress, where power over trade policy in Washington resides, or to exercise much effective control over decisions vital to our commerce at home and abroad. Even were the American Congress to extend an invitation to us to join NAFTA, which I much doubt, I do not believe that it would be attractive to a people as intensely pragmatic as the British, who can see its drawbacks. The UK would have a good deal less effective sovereignty than it has now.

The second proposition commands much wider support and has a rather higher chance of happening, so it deserves a more detailed response. If for most sceptics the issue is not about leaving the EU, but about the basis on which we stay in it, what about their assertions? And what about the things they omit to mention?

Let us take first the objections relating to the role and extent of public sector intervention in the economy. Suffice to say here that sceptics frequently exaggerate the extent of UK liberalization as compared with her EU partners and they have no evidence for the implicit assertion that the situation in the rest of Europe is getting worse. On the contrary, four interacting secular changes are under way which will undermine these politico-economic objections by transforming and liberalizing the EU single market beyond all recognition: the market liberalization and reform agenda agreed at the Lisbon summit; the full entry into force of the single currency; the enlargement of the EU to admit new members with highly competitive industries and services; and, finally, globalization. Taken together, these will go to make up a dynamic private sector in the European continent fully competitive on a global basis.

It may be argued that the UK can have the advantage of all of these without belonging to the single currency itself. This is not true. The current advantages of investing in the UK will increasingly be outweighed by the attractions of better market conditions across the channel and the draw-backs of our geography combined with the costs and risks associated with our separate currency. Over time the effects would be serious and not just commercial. The eurogroup governments, charged with developing policy on the wider economic consequences of the single mone-tary area, will soon develop considerable influence over the future direction of the single market. The distinction made by some eurosceptics between market-related and non market-related integration will thus make decreasing sense. And, as a non-member of the eurozone, the UK will not be in on the design stage of this new phase. The disad-vantages of this to the UK will not be hidden to third coun-tries either, who will know that power on certain issues central to the EU's development lies elsewhere than

London. It is hard to see how becoming a taker rather than a maker of policy on central issues would assist in solving the sceptics' perceived dilemma of 'being in Europe but not run by it'. It is much more likely to leave the UK stranded.

One might also query the point of staying out of such a single currency. It would be a pretty odd use of British sovereignty to deny to British companies and the British economy the advantages of full membership of a dynamic single market. Unless, of course, one thinks that national independence is more important than national welfare and must, if necessary, be purchased at the price of it. That is not the view the UK has taken for over 50 years on defence. We have consistently derided the French abstention from a key bit of NATO decision-making machinery, the integrated military structure, for letting nationalism get in the way of an enlightened view of the national interest.

No country lives for long in a relaxed and confident way if it does not possess a consensus on where it is heading. This is true of the UK today. Arguments over our place in the EU bite into the fabric of our national politics. Prolonged uncertainty, which business strongly dislikes, saps national drive and unity more generally.

Devolution has generated energy and a local sense of purpose in Scotland which is missing, and to some extent resented, in England. Europhobia, in part an expression of frustrated national identity, is significantly stronger in England than in other parts of our own union. Scotland is more europhile than England. In Northern Ireland the economic disadvantages of not being in the same currency zone as the Republic become ever more obvious as economic growth, productivity, and living standards in the Republic rise steadily above those in the north. The tensions inside our union are not likely to be allayed by prolonged delay on the euro question. And a negative outcome would be likely to increase underlying centrifugal tendencies. Perceptions (and realities) concerning the benefits of the EU are not evenly spread through the UK and we should bear in mind that in the last analysis there is a link between the cohesiveness of our own union and decisions we take about the extent of our participation in the EU.

Over time failure to join the eurozone would diminish the UK's power in the wider world—in particular in transatlantic relations, which have a greater importance for us than for either Germany or France, since they are part of our international power base. Quite a bit of our pulling power in the world stems from the widespread (and correct) perception that there is a deeper degree of understanding and a closer degree of active cooperation on a very broad front between London and Washington than between America and her other allies. But this will not survive on either side unless judged to serve a useful purpose. The brutal fact is that for the US, much as the EU may be a source of spasmodic irritation and dismay, and sometimes of serious transatlantic disagreement, European integration remains an important objective in its own right as a way of stabilizing relations between former European enemies and underpinning the emerging democracies of Central and Eastern Europe.

For the realization of this goal, the US has fostered the emergence of another trading bloc and economic power-house this side of the Atlantic (in which they invest), and they want Europeans to pick up more of the tab of political action and responsibility. Put simply, the EU is more important to America than the special relationship with the UK on its own. The conclusion for the UK is clear: far from being a zero-sum game, being more closely integrated in Europe does not mean less influence for the UK with the US. Less power in Europe would mean less influence for the UK in Washington.

We have to recognize some of the facts of power in the twenty-first century for what they are. The UK does not wield a great deal of power and influence on her own. We can choose an offshore role, but it will bring with it steady diminution of influence in other things we care about. We need to be clear-sighted about the distinction in real life between formal sovereignty and effective power, which may be shared. As a leading outward-looking European power, we can exert quite a lot of influence, deploying the collective muscle of our partners as well as our own. We have a clear track record of success here which it makes little sense to cede gratuitously.

SOVEREIGNTY AND DEMOCRACY
John Redwood

One currency needs one government

If you want a democratic country it needs its own currency. One people, one governing system, one central bank, one currency: these go together.

The whole debate has been clouded by a common confusion between sovereignty and power. It is quite true that if you set up a small country with its own currency it will have less power to direct its own future than a large country. The USA has much more power and influence in the world than Estonia. Nonetheless, it is still possible for Estonia as well as the USA to be a sovereign country.

Not even the mighty USA is all-powerful. If the USA wishes to take action which has an impact on countries anywhere around the world it has to listen to world public opinion, it has to be diplomatic, it has to play by international rules laid down by international bodies, and has to accept that there are limits even to its own colossal power. A small country may have to make more accommodations with its neighbours than a very large one. A small economy with its own currency may have a great deal of power and influence to direct its own affairs or if it is heavily dependent upon the trade and influence of its neighbours it may find its options are more limited. This is not the same as saying that it has ceased to be sovereign.

By way of an analogy, once the government has raided my wage packet I am sovereign to decide how to spend what remains. I have control of my own bank account. Only I can place money in and take money out of the account. I am not all-powerful. I do not have much bargaining power in the market to get discounts which I would get if I went shopping in conjunction with my neighbours and made block purchases with them. There are some things that are too expensive for an individual to buy which he would be able to afford if he clubbed together with his neighbours. However, this lack of buying power does not make me wish to give up the sovereignty over my own bank account.

I would have more power collectively if I and all my neighbours pooled together our bank account monies and decided on common purchasing. We do not do so, because we recognize that we would not enjoy the extra power as much as we would be annoyed by the lack of control over what we ourselves had put in. How would we agree on what we all wanted to buy, and when? I would rather be sovereign than share in more power. So it is with a nation.

A nation has its own bank account and its own currency. The country's elected government decides on the movements into and out of the account. Foreign exchange reserves of the country are under the direction of the central bank, which is in turn under the direction of the central government and elected parliament. If the country makes a good job of managing its financial affairs, its neighbours have little control or influence over it. If the country makes a bad job and needs to turn to the international community to borrow, then it has less power and influence over its future. The fact that a country may make mistakes and may manage its own affairs badly is not sufficiently good reason for that country to volunteer to give up all individual say and sway over its financial affairs.

The democratic deficit

Those who argue the case for more European integration often point to a democratic deficit in the way the current European institutions work. They are quite right in pointing out that the European Commission, aided and abetted by the Council of Ministers, legislates for more than 350 million people in Western Europe without proper democratic scrutiny, argument, or parliamentary debate.

The situation in monetary and economic policy is in some ways even worse. The EU has decided upon a method of running the single currency which is secretive and bureaucratic. Based upon a misunderstanding of how the German system worked in the post-war period, the European Central Bank has sole charge over interest rates, the stock of money, and the general conduct of monetary policy. This body is directed by a group of board members of the Central Bank governing body who are appointed for long single terms, who are not answerable to any elected parliament, and who are effectively in place for the duration however they perform or behave.

In a democracy like Britain's some of the most important debates usually take place about the conduct of economic policy. In post-war Britain general elections have usually been about economic management or mismanagement. If one party feels that the government has chosen the wrong interest rates, has spent too much, borrowed too much or taxed too much, they try to make this the dominant issue in the election campaign. It can make or break the government. Democratic process gives a safety valve to businesspeople and the public in the event that they feel the economy has been badly run.

In the case of the European Central Bank there will always be a permanent democratic deficit. Were the European Central Bank to set interest rates that were too high and to restrict money policy too severely, there will be mass unemployment, too many bankruptcies, and a low level of business activity across Western Europe. The people who carried out this policy would be unassailable. No vote cast in a general election anywhere in a member state could make one iota of difference to the conduct of this policy or to the people who were undertaking it. Similarly, if the Board of the Central Bank misjudge things the other way, set interest rates that were too low, printed too much money, and created a big inflation, there would be nothing the population of the member states could do.

Those who favour more European integration often use the democratic deficit argument about law-making to urge the case for the European Parliament itself having more power. It is quite true that one solution to the obvious democratic deficit in the Community would be to give the European Parliament the necessary powers to propose, amend, countermand, and enact legislation. Similarly, in the economic scheme the European Parliament could be given the power to interrogate and if necessary remove from office the board members of the Central Bank if the economic policy they were pursuing was not meeting the demands of enough people throughout the EU.

Architects of a federal Europe rarely want proper parliamentary control over the banking and monetary policies of the Community. They believe that bureaucrats are always better at these things than elected representatives and seem to distrust any democratic safety valve. Still, the idea that the European Parliament should be given more law-making powers would make a lot of sense if you wish to see a United States of Europe created. My view is that the peoples of Western Europe are certainly not ready to be governed as one. The languages, cultures, interests, and outlooks are so divergent that there is no overwhelming desire to bring them all together under one strong centralized control. There is no clear political community throughout Western Europe and not even as yet well-organized transnational parties. There is every evidence to suppose that the more centralized bureaucratic power is strengthened in the EU, the more nationalist and sub-nationalist movements will develop, angry at the lack of proper consultation or democratic influence over the centre.

Isn't the independent Bank of England just like the independent European Central Bank?

In recent years there have been moves to create more bureaucratic independence in British monetary and interest rate policy. The Bank of England governors are now charged with the task of settling interest rates on the advice of their Monetary Committee, and the chancellor of the exchequer claims that he will no longer meddle with this system. However, there is a big difference between the so-called independence of the Bank of England and the genuine independence so far of the European Central Bank. The members of the UK Monetary Committee can be removed by the chancellor of the exchequer and are clearly under some political influence as the politicians choose the targets and the guidelines to be issued overall to the Bank. The Bank of England's independence has been created by statute, by Act of Parliament. If this government or some future government gets disenchanted with the results of this semi-independence, then it can be swept away in an afternoon of legislative activity in the House of Commons. If the Bank of England made enough mistakes, bankrupted enough people, or drove inflation up too far, there would be a strong democratic pressure to change the system. Any sensible government would give in to such pressure.

In the case of the European Central Bank it is difficult to see how such forces could find a legitimate democratic outlet. It would require major Treaty change in order to make the Bank more susceptible to democratic opinion.

Is there an optimum area for a single currency?

The optimum area for any single currency is the area that represents a political nation. Single currencies go well with single markets where those markets are unified by a common language and a common outlook. As all single currency areas deliver the wrong interest rates and the wrong exchange rates for some parts of them, it is most important that there should be relative freedom of movement of people, talent, ideas, and capital around the entire single currency area. The bigger the single currency area the more towns, cities, regions, and nations end up with the wrong interest rates and the wrong amount of money in circulation. The larger the area the more need there is for compensating flows of money in the form of grants, subsidies, benefits, and investment to try to offset the dislocation which a wrong exchange rate or interest rate so readily creates.

It is most important that people think those taking the decisions on their behalf have legitimacy and authority. If a single currency area is made too large and then people in part of that area start to suffer as a result it can lead to questioning of authority itself. This is especially likely where the people making the decisions are not even elected by the wider electorate in the greater currency union area, let alone directly responsive to the people living in the part of the currency area that is being damaged by the common policy.

Conclusions

There is a dangerous democratic deficit in the EU. It would be possible to cure the deficit for new legislation if people consented to a superstate and wanted to charge its parliament with the sole power of proposing and making laws. The reluctance of people to do this is a sure sign that the peoples of Western Europe are not ready to live in a superstate and do not regard the European level as the legitimate source of authority and power in their community.

An even worse democratic problem will emerge with the single currency. An independent Central Bank will mean growing frustration in those parts of the single currency area where unemployment remains obstinately high or where inflation takes off. The single currency area is far too large for there to be a single interest rate and a single exchange rate which is right for all.

If people do not consent to powerful individuals at the European level settling most of the important matters about their economic future then the scheme is in the long term doomed. The EU understands that it will need to control budget deficits and therefore the overall levels of spending and taxation in the captive economies of

Euroland. They also wish to gain much more control and influence over the powers of taxation. They intend to do this by negotiation and by bureaucratic means. The more they succeed, the more they stifle the democratic lifeblood of Western Europe, and the more danger there is that the people will rebel and demand a return to legitimate democratic national government.

5 EUROPE AND THE WORLD

Towards the end of 2000 the EU member states spelt out the contribution they were each prepared to make to the European Rapid Reaction Force. It is intended that this should be ready by 2003 for carrying out peacekeeping and humanitarian tasks in response to international crises. The impetus for the Force and for Europe to have an autonomous military capability stems from the joint British–French declaration at St Malo in 1998. This is the most concrete development yet in the field of Common Foreign and Security Policy (CFSP), which was established as a 'pillar' of the EU by the Maastricht Treaty in 1992. Maastricht superseded previous attempts to coordinate foreign and defence policy across Europe, which had had little success. The creation of the new Force has caused con-troversy, with critics concerned that it could lead towards undermining NATO and decoupling the US from European security. There are also wider questions about Europe's role in the world and long-term relationship with the US.

THE FOREIGN POLICY CHALLENGE
Lord Owen

The overriding challenge in the foreign and defence field for EU member states has not changed much from what I wrote at the end of 1995, after having spent nearly three years negotiating on behalf of the EU in the former Yugoslavia: 'they have never exercised power: in part because they believed that they did not have sufficient power to exercise without the participation of the US, in part because the EU does not yet know how to exercise power.'

After the humiliating dependence of the EU on the US during NATO's action in Serbia and Kosovo, and with the experience of the UN in Bosnia, Tony Blair correctly decided that the EU had to build the structures appropriate to the exercising of military power in circumstances when the US in the future might not wish to undertake military action. He joined with President Jacques Chirac at St Malo in calling for 'the capacity for autonomous action, backed up by credible military forces, the means to decide to use them, and a readiness to do so, in order to respond to international crises'. The messy results of their initiative became all too clear in the run-up to the Nice summit, and the wording did not even have the endorsement of NATO. Now with President George W Bush in office with a highly experienced cabinet there is a fresh opportunity to negotiate a much better balanced NATO/EU relationship.

Some believe that the Rapid Reaction Force should be confined to the European theatre. I am not so convinced about this. I can see circumstances in the next decade where America might not wish to deploy troops in central Asia, for example, in and around Chechnya, but where a European force might just be acceptable. There could be places in Africa where, following US experience in Somalia and their refusal to involve the UN in Rwanda, there would be no political support in the Security Council from America for a UN force, but where they would be ready to help, though not to take part in, the deployment of a European force in which they would have more confidence.

One of the questions over the European Rapid Reaction Force is that some people see autonomy as consisting not just in deploying without American troops although with American goodwill, but also in deploying against the wishes of the US. Such a deployment could never be contemplated other than in a dire situation, and in these circumstances Europe would almost certainly be wiser to plan for stand-off diplomacy and rule out military engagement. To plan in Europe for deploying troops against the interests of a settled ally like the US is not prudent but provocative, as well as being corrosive of the most essential element, trust.

When the Berlin Wall collapsed in 1989 there was much loose talk that NATO had been made redundant. The invasion of Kuwait by Iraq in 1991 and ethnic cleansing in Bosnia and Kosovo reaffirmed the strength of having not just US forces on the ground in Europe but also the value of a working multilateral framework for military consultation and action. This should be particularly compelling for those who view US superpower unilateralism as a cause for concern.

When the then US secretary of defense William Cohen warned Europe in December 2000 that NATO would become a relic if the EU developed its own forces, some in Europe believed that NATO was already a relic and that its rationale had died with the end of the Soviet Union. Before that type of thinking takes a grip on the centre-left in the UK, let alone in Europe, we need to recall a few historic moments for Europe. The US military came in on the ground in the First World War as late as April 1917. Only after Pearl Harbour was attacked by the Japanese in December 1941 could as strong a president as Franklin Roosevelt come into the Second World War. Suez in 1956 should also be a continuing lesson for those who hunger for Europe to take military action outside its own immediate sphere of influence against the wishes of the US.

Even had Europe been ready to take military action against Serbia in relation to Kosovo in 1999 and the US not deployed troops, it would have been essential to have had American/NATO resources. Yet even with full US political support, and the reduced political weight and the depletion of Russian military forces, Europe's political resolve and military forces would have been insufficient to have triumphed over Milosevic without US armed forces. Realistically, that situation is likely to continue through the twenty-first century. The EU will not have the sense of unity and identity or the political coherence to develop or to wield the power of a superpower, for, unlike the US, it does not have the single authority that stems from being a single democratic nation; nor should it attempt to become a superpower.

The reasons are complex. Europe has been over many centuries an economic powerhouse, but, even with the useful addition of building our unique Union of inter-governmentalism and supranationalism, over the last 45 years we have little appetite for becoming a superpower. Historically it is not just the political attitudes that gave rise to appeasement in the 1930s or the unilateral nuclear disarmament campaigns of the 1970s and 1980s. One only has to remember that both the government of Italy and prominent people in the German government called publicly for a bombing pause within days of NATO's airstrikes against Serbia in 1999. Had those demands been accepted by America, the UK, and France, the certain consequence would have been that the bombing would not have resumed and Milosevic would have won.

Looking today at the future pattern of work in the EU's Common Foreign and Security Policy, the focus will be on Russia and this must be the correct priority. Russian territory will border the EU when Poland and Estonia become members. The Russian exclave of Kaliningrad, which is enclosed by Lithuania and Poland, represents a potential focus of tension between the EU and Russia, and it is very important that we help to diversify the Kaliningrad economy from a solely military one to make it a commercial trading port and hinterland. Russia will always expect to be treated as a great nation, and as part of this it seems wise to hold open the prospect of eventual EU membership, but with little likelihood that they will wish to take up the option. The US has difficulty in sustaining a steady economic and strategic relationship with Russia, whereas the EU, using all its institutions in a coordinated programme, has the interest that stems from knowing that we cannot distance ourselves from each other when we are inescapably bound together as citizens of one continent.

Working more effectively with Turkey and nurturing Turkish aspirations for an earlier entry into the EU than most of the Brussels elite think feasible is also a priority, given the politics of the accession of Cyprus. The UN is currently in the lead diplomatically over Cyprus, but we need in addition a 'Contact Group' approach of no more than six nations, as was successful over Namibia and still operates in the Balkans. In this case it should involve Turkey and Greece, the UK and the US, France and Germany.

Perhaps the most pressing issue that will impact on both defence and foreign policy in Europe is the new American administration's obvious determination to go ahead with the technological and scientific investment for a ballistic missile defence system. The wiser European political leaders will take this priority as a fact of life rather than trying to block it. For the UK the upgrading of US radars in this country, as part of any US missile defence system, presents political problems with a significant section of public opinion. Unlike America we have never had a politician of Reagan's simple directness explaining why defence based on shooting down incoming nuclear missiles is far better than defence based on retaliating with nuclear missiles. We went into Mutual and Assured Destruction (MAD) as a deterrent strategy for NATO because there was no technological alternative available, not because we thought retaliation an inherently stable response. There may be no technological breakthrough on ballistic missile defence, but for the US to explore the possibility need not be as politically destabilizing as some predict, particularly if it is genuinely part of an overall disarmament package. It is extremely important that this potentially divisive area between NATO member states does not coincide with rumbling discontent in the US over the EU's new defence policy.

I remain optimistic about the basic American–European relationship and the important role in that relationship for the UK – provided, and this is a major proviso, that the UK maintains its identity as a self-governing nation. Some genuinely believe that the self-governing nature of the member states within the EU is not in doubt. We will be better able to judge that after the 2004 Inter-Governmental Conference, and meanwhile we should stay opted out of the euro.

From a ringside seat in the Council of Foreign Ministers from 1977 to 1979 and from being invited to almost every Council of Foreign Ministers meeting between 1992 and 1995, I have watched the process of political cooperation in the European Community grow into a Common Foreign and Security Policy in the EU. It was staggering to see the gains made in the habit of consultation during the 13-year gap. Slowly the EU is developing the cohesion that NATO has developed at both official and ministerial level—with only consensual decision-making. Let us hope that we will hear no more about member states being expected to drop their last resort veto on foreign and defence policy within the EU by embracing qualified majority voting.

WHY EUROPE NEEDS ITS OWN DEFENCE FORCE

Charles Grant

For most of its 50-year history, the EU has been essentially about economics. Over the coming decades, however, many of the Union's challenges will be external: how to enlarge into Eastern Europe; how to ensure the peace, prosperity, and stability of the countries which remain beyond the EU's frontiers; and how to reinvigorate a transatlantic relationship that must adapt to the EU's becoming, in some respects, a major power.

The Union's member states are trying hard to build a more effective and coherent Common Foreign and Security Policy (CFSP). The 15 governments are backing a plan for the Union to develop the means to deploy a Rapid Reaction Force of 60,000 troops, and to sustain it in the field for a year. The governments believe that this force will improve the Union's ability to manage crises in places such as the Balkans. One of the reasons why unseemly rulers have often ignored the Union's pronouncements is that they have assumed—rightly—that the Union was all bark and no bite.

The EU has already created new institutions, designed to help implement the common defence policy. But the significance of this defence initiative, as opposed to earlier, still-born efforts to give the EU a role in defence, is that it is more about military capabilities than new institutions. The British government understood that the best way to get the Americans on board was to show them that the point of the new policy was to enhance the capacity of the Europeans to deploy militarily useful forces outside the NATO area. Hence in December 1999 the EU governments set themselves a 'Headline Goal', defining the kinds of troops and equipment that would be needed for an effective Rapid Reaction Force.

It is too early to reach any definitive conclusions, but the combination of the Headline Goal plus peer-group pressure among the member states does seem to be having an effect. During 2001, the defence budgets of Britain, Denmark, Greece, Italy, Luxembourg, the Netherlands, Portugal, and Spain are set to rise in real terms. And more important, governments are spending a greater part of their defence budgets on the sorts of equipment that are needed for crisis-management missions; France, for example, has increased spending on weapons procurement for 2001.

Many sceptics in the US and in Europe do not see the point of all this effort and expenditure. Why bother, when NATO is already there and it works quite well? Should not the EU stick to economics and leave defence to an organization that is, to a large extent, run by the Americans?

There are three possible answers to these questions. The first is to say that Europe needs its own defence so that it can stand up to the US. A stronger CFSP would allow the EU to resist US hegemony and prevent the sole super-power from steamrollering the rest of the world. To judge from much of what has been written in the British media, European defence is a French trap—designed to undermine NATO and poison Britain's special relationship with the US—into which a naïve Tony Blair has fallen head first.

Now it is true that a minority of French Gaullists, and some left-wingers in other parts of Europe, do support European defence for anti-American reasons. But these people are not in power and have not been responsible for negotiating the future of European defence. The politicians and diplomats running the show would give two other answers to the above questions.

One is idealist: because European integration is an inherently good thing, anything that promotes common defence policies must be desirable. The other answer is pragmatic: given the many challenges and interests that the member states share in common, they can often achieve more in foreign and defence policy through working together than alone.

These two answers, although very different, are in no way incompatible with each other. The British government's motivation for thinking up the Headline Goal—the first example in the history of the EU of Britain taking a major initiative and its partners following—was pragmatic. Some of the other governments are more idealist, but they have nevertheless been spurred on by a strong perception of their own self-interest. The Kosovo crisis of spring 1999, in particular, highlighted the need for more effective European foreign policies and military capabilities: every EU government wanted to get the Albanian refugees back to their homes, and every government knew that NATO's air campaign depended to a large extent on US technology and expertise. On their own, the Europeans could not have coped with the Kosovo crisis.

The basis of the pragmatic case for European defence is the striking convergence of the principal foreign policy interests of the big European states in recent decades. Germany is behaving much more like other European countries: it refused to get involved in the Gulf War, but now has peacekeeping troops in Bosnia and Kosovo. France has moved much closer to NATO and, during the Kosovo air campaign, put its forces under American command. Blair's Britain has moved closer to Europe while Italy's communists have become mainstream social democrats.

The Balkan crises of the 1990s helped the European governments to appreciate how many interests they shared. Under the command of first the United Nations and then NATO, forces from many EU countries worked well together in pursuit of common objectives. The Europeans hope that the Americans will remain committed to NATO's peacekeeping operations in the Balkans. However, as President Bush has indicated, the US may not keep its troops there indefinitely. All the more reason for the Europeans to prepare for the eventuality that Big Brother may not be there to hold their hands.

The EU's plans envisage three sorts of military mission which could involve European troops. One would be a conventional NATO force. In the event of a serious shooting war, all the Europeans would want the whole of NATO to be engaged. The second would be an EU force, for a mission that NATO and the US supported, but for which the US would not want to commit troops. The EU force would draw upon NATO command structures and planning capabilities, as well as American equipment, but consist of only European troops. In normal circumstances, the EU governments would need this kind of assistance, for they still lack important but essential military capabilities—for example, the ability to shift heavy cargo by air or to suppress enemy air defences.

The third option is for an EU force that would be able to operate autonomously, without NATO support. But what is the need for an option which—given the current level of European capabilities—is likely to be hypothetical for many years to come? The answer is that unless the Europeans make an effort to build the capacity to operate autonomously, they will never succeed in developing the military means that would allow them to become more useful partners in NATO. If they presumed that they could always count on the US to provide the wherewithal, they would find every excuse to cut defence budgets and substitute fine rhetoric for hard capabilities.

No European government is proposing to duplicate America's fleet of stealthy B-2 bombers or its huge intelligence-gathering networks. The kinds of autonomy to which the Europeans aspire are principally in unglamorous areas such as air and sea transport, the ability to deploy a corps headquarters, or the provision of adequate maintenance and support for fighter squadrons that are stationed away from home.

The historical significance of the European defence initiative is certainly huge; but for the foreseeable future the practical changes to the way the EU works will in fact be modest. The EU institutions will not have any decision-making powers on European defence. All decisions on the deployment of troops will be by unanimity, which means that each EU country can wield a veto. The Commission will not be involved.

The total size of the EU's military staff in the Council of Ministers Secretariat will be just over one hundred. This staff will advise the ministers and national diplomats based in Brussels, and liase with other bodies such as NATO. But the EU will not set up its own staff of operational planners: it will draw on the planning expertise of its own military planning staff: it will draw on the planning expertise of either NATO or the member states. Similarly, the EU will not have its own command structures, but will draw on those of NATO, multinational headquarters (such as the Eurocorps), or the member states.

This defence initiative is not about weakening NATO, but strengthening it. All the capabilities that the Europeans succeed in developing will be made available to NATO. That is why most of George W Bush's advisers support the European defence initiative. They understand that if the Headline Goal is fulfilled, the Europeans will be more useful allies. There is certainly scepticism in Washington that the Europeans will be able to deliver on the capabilities. But there is an acknowledgement that NATO, as an organization, has failed to badger its European members to do much about capabilities, and that the EU—as a club which most of its members take very seriously—may stand a better chance. At the time of writing, every NATO member bar Turkey has approved the EU's plans for the Rapid Reaction Force.

If the Europeans can make a success of their Rapid Reaction Force, the EU will have moved a little way towards becoming—in Tony Blair's words—'a superpower, but not a superstate'. This will require some rebalancing of the transatlantic relationship. The Americans would no longer complain so much about the Europeans being unwilling to share the burden of looking after their own security. They would need to learn the habit of consulting their allies more often. But the reward for the US would be considerable: an EU that was a more useful partner in helping it to sort out the world's security crises.

THE PROBLEMS FOR NATO
Sir Michael Armitage

It was perhaps inevitable that, as the EU developed, the long-standing wish for a purely European defence capability would be revived. This time a specific plan is on the table. In 1999 the creation of a European Rapid Reaction Force was agreed, and in November 2000 more precise proposals took shape. The most important of these was that the new force should be totally separate from NATO, which would mean a fundamental break from over 50 years of successful western defence cooperation.

There was widespread criticism of the new force both from Labour and Tory sources. Such well-informed figures as Lord Healey, Lord Owen, Lord Carrington, Sir Malcolm Rifkind, Lord Robertson, Baroness Thatcher, the then US defense secretary William Cohen, and Jesse Helms, the veteran chairman of the US Senate Committee on Foreign Relations, all expressed serious misgivings about the likely effect of the new force on NATO.

Other critics have pointed out that the force is to be made up of existing European defence assets, most of which are already assigned to NATO. In another complication, some of these assets are at the same time engaged in UN peacekeeping tasks, while in the particular case of the UK our forces also have purely national responsibilities such as those in Cyprus and the Falklands. A situation of simultaneous crises on all four fronts, as it were, is extremely unlikely, but that is not the whole story. Military commitments involve not only operational deployment away from base and often overseas, but deployments away from base for training as well. Yet already the degree of overstretch in the armed forces of the UK is causing unacceptably long periods of separation for families, contributing in no small way to worrying re-engagement figures, and probably to the very disappointing levels of recruiting as well. The new force must not become another burden.

Another criticism of the proposed European force arises from the question of command and control. Assuming the worst case, that is to say a full European force deployment of around 60,000 troops plus major sea and air components, then there are two command, control, and communications (C3) possibilities. First, the existing NATO command structure and technical infrastructure might be used. But in that case the considerable number of Americans in NATO's integrated military staff would presumably stand aside to be replaced by Europeans. This idea might work, even though it is not clear where these replacements would come from. A far more serious obstacle to this proposal, however, is that France is adamantly opposed to it. France is insisting on a quite separate European force C3 structure.

The second possibility would be to create new headquarters staffs and infrastructures at all levels more or less in parallel to the integrated military staff of NATO. This would mean a very large manpower bill, and very substantial new investment in communications and other infrastructure. Given the pressures on national defence budgets, and the almost universal reluctance to increase them, this manpower and this infrastructure could be found only at the expense of existing assets. Yet there is no slack in NATO with which to absorb these new demands. The result of setting up an entirely independent C3 structure would thus be to drain European resources away from NATO, which would either gravely weaken its ability to function or throw even more of a burden onto the Americans.

There are also complications for the European force at the political level. Turkey, with her strategic position between the uncertainties of south-west Europe and the instabilities of the Middle East, is one of them. She belongs to NATO but not to the EU. In her particular case it is some comfort to know that an accommodation has been found by the acceptance of her offer of up to 6,000 personnel and a number of tactical aircraft for the new force. And no doubt the next accessions to NATO, that is to say the Czech Republic, Hungary, and Poland, will somehow be absorbed into the NATO command structure.

But the agreement to contribute to the force by nations that are neither EU nor NATO members, in this case Bulgaria, Cyprus, Estonia, Latvia, Lithuania, Malta,

Romania, Slovakia, and Slovenia, seems likely to add greatly to the many problems of coordination, standardization, and, in the end, harmony and unanimity in any future ventures — problems that NATO itself overcame only in the face of a very clear and serious military threat. This prospect of a wide and growing inclusiveness in the absence of such a threat needs to be most carefully weighted against the grave penalty that NATO will almost certainly have to pay for it, namely the loss of US participation.

Most of the criticism of the new force has concerned itself with this prospect. Since the very earliest days of NATO, Europe has relied heavily on the military and industrial strength of the US. This was perhaps largely to do with nuclear weapons, but it also covered the whole range of other military capabilities, including manpower, which the nations of Europe were unwilling or unable to devote to their own defence. This is no less true today. For example, as the Commons Defence Select Committee stated in its report in October 2000, Europe's response to the Kosovo crisis was admitted to have been 'abysmal'. The fact is that European NATO has nothing like the enormous airlift capability of the US; it does not have anything like the huge US arsenal of high-precision weapons; but above all, and with the exception of the UK, European NATO completely lacks the extraordinary intelligence-gathering assets that are available to the US.

This question of shared intelligence is the issue on which almost all else in the debate about the European force will eventually hinge. It is generally well known that the US, Canada, and Britain share their most sensitive intelligence, and that it is from this source that NATO in turn largely derives its own intelligence assessments. If the new European force were to operate outside NATO's planning umbrella, the Americans would rightly fear very damaging intelligence leakages, such as that alleged to have occurred during the Kosovo crisis, when NATO targeting intentions where apparently finding their way to Belgrade.

As Iain Duncan Smith, the Conservative defence spokesman, said recently, 'The Cold War was won by the diplomacy of Ronald Reagan and Margaret Thatcher, backed at all times by the amazing capabilities of the American reconnaissance and navigation satellites coupled with GCHQ at Cheltenham. It meant we knew what they were up to . . . To dazzle Europe with the belief that any EU force could operate successfully — no matter how good the forces are — without this transatlantic intelligence bridge is putting lives at risk and deluding the people of Britain.' The apparent French belief that Europe in general, and France in particular, might be able to replace the breath and depth of this vital US intelligence capability is simply breathtaking.

The fundamental difficulty with the new European force is that it is an 'openly political project', as Lords Healey, Owen, and Carrington and Sir Malcolm Rifkind pointed out in a recent letter to the Daily Telegraph. Or, as former US Assistant Defense Secretary Richard Perle has said, it is a monument to France's 'towering conceit'. Certainly

France sees it as a means of reducing American influence in Europe, and seems blind to the danger that, as William Cohen has said, 'the Atlantic alliance would become a relic of the past'. Little thought seems to have been given either to the purely military dimension of the project, or, despite a chorus of warning voices from both sides of the Atlantic, to its wider political implications.

Is there a way forward? That will depend upon the kind of tasks that the new force will be expected to undertake. It has already been made clear in official announcements that the force will not be a war-fighting one; its remit will confine it to humanitarian and peacekeeping missions. In that case, the problems it will face will be largely administrative rather than purely military (and logistics are already a national rather than a NATO responsibility). Such limited missions should not be unduly demanding in terms of staff effort. In the event of a crisis, it should therefore be a simple matter, well within the 60 days' maximum specified, to form an ad hoc purely European C3 structure using NATO resources and operating within them.

The only permanent staff required by the force would be that needed to monitor the content of the 'capabilities catalogue'. This ad hoc and limited approach will be the only way in which the transatlantic intelligence links can be retained, and the alliance itself saved from disintegration.

6 AGRICULTURE AND FISHING

The Common Agricultural Policy is the most expensive item in the European Union budget, accounting for nearly half the EU's total spending. The CAP guarantees minimum prices to farmers, with the EU intervening to buy up surplus stock as well as subsidizing exports and imposing tariffs on imports of agricultural produce from outside the EU. The CAP has been heavily criticized, for reasons which include its cost, the high price of food which results, the 'butter mountains' and 'wine lakes' of stockpiled surplus produce which it has generated, the level of fraud, the environmental impact of intensive farming, and its souring of relations with many non-EU countries. But for its supporters it has boosted farming productivity, protected European food supplies, and increased quality and variety.

Attempts have been made over the years to reform the CAP, but it has proved difficult to win the support necessary for them to be implemented. However, in 1992 the agriculture commissioner, Ray MacSharry, succeeded in persuading the member states to reduce some guaranteed prices and move instead towards direct payments to farmers, for example, to take land out of production. Further cuts in guaranteed prices and other changes were introduced in 1999 as part of the Commission's 'Agenda 2000' proposals. Nevertheless, the CAP still faces forceful demands for reform, both because of the prospect of EU enlargement and also because of pressure from the World Trade Organization over its protectionist aspects.

The Common Fisheries Policy regulates access to and preservation of fishing stocks. Only a very small proportion of the EU population are involved in the fishing industry, but the CFP has a direct and powerful impact on them. It has been the source of much bitterness and controversy in Britain.

NONSENSICALITIES AND DISASTERS

Christopher Booker

What will people eat when all the fish are caught and all the cattle slaughtered?

Maxim Gorky, *Three Of Them*

Let us begin with two decisions taken in Brussels just before Christmas 2000, under the Common Agricultural Policy and the Common Fisheries Policy respectively.

The first, in the wake of the BSE scare spreading to the continent, was an EU-wide extension of the scheme, pioneered in Britain, to kill and incinerate all cattle over 30 months old, apart from milking cows. Even when this scheme was first introduced in Britain at the height of the 1996 BSE panic, it was not supported by scientific advice. It was launched at the instigation of the supermarkets to 'restore consumer confidence'. But there was still less reason, despite the renewed hysteria which built up over BSE in the autumn of 2000, to extend the scheme to the rest of the EU. The result, at a cost of untold billions of pounds to EU taxpayers, will eventually be to send tens of millions of healthy animals up in smoke, to no practical purpose whatever.

The second decision was intended to remedy the dramatic recent collapse in North Sea stocks of fish such as cod and haddock. Under their 'cod recovery scheme', Commission officials imposed crippling restrictions on fishing over a vast area of the North Sea. But there was to be no restriction on so-called 'industrial fishing' in the same area. This allows a mainly Danish trawler fleet to use tiny meshed nets to sweep up more than one million tonnes a year of smaller fish such as sand eels and pout, to be used as agricultural fertilizer or to provide food for Denmark's intensive pig and poultry industries.

Not only do these smaller fish provide the main food source for the larger fish, so that many experts believe the devastating impact of industrial fishing has in fact been a key factor in the disappearance of North Sea cod and haddock, but the industrial trawlers are also allowed a 20 per cent 'by-catch' of cod, haddock, and other larger fish, amounting to more than 200,000 tonnes of the very species the recovery scheme is intended to protect. While Scottish fishermen face such restrictions on landing cod for human consumption that they predict more than half the Scottish fleet, 500 vessels, may soon be driven out of business, it is considered perfectly acceptable for the Danes to catch far more cod than the Scots are allowed, so long as it is spread on fields or fed to pigs.

It would be easy to cite dozens of similar instances of the bizarre nonsensicalities which the CAP and the CFP so often produce in practice. In theory the declared intentions of both policies may seem to have much to commend them. But to anyone unfamiliar with their detailed workings it is almost impossible to convey just what a terrifying gap has opened up between aspiration and practice.

There has been no more devastating analysis of the CAP than a memorandum presented by the Ministry of Agriculture, Fisheries and Food (MAFF) to a House of Lords committee in 1995. This pointed out how the five aims of the CAP are set out in the Treaty of Rome, from providing farmers with a reasonable standard of living to supplying consumers with food at reasonable prices. On all five counts, MAFF concluded, this vastly expensive attempt to impose a common system on agriculture from the Arctic Circle to Andalucia had failed, creating a social, economic, and environmental disaster.

By promoting ever larger units and ever more intensive farming methods, the CAP has been a major factor in destroying wildlife. Across Europe it has driven millions of smaller farmers to the wall. Its subsidy system, paying out huge sums to some sectors and none to others, has piled up vast quantities of unwanted produce. It has provided opportunities for almost limitless fraud. By subsidized dumping it has inflicted untold damage on the economies of the third world. And all this to make food for Western Europe's 370 million consumers not cheaper but £1000 a year more expensive per family than it might have been otherwise.

Again, in theory, the CFP's aim to merge all Western Europe's fishing waters into one 'common resource' and to conserve fish stocks by parcelling out permissible catches between different nations may sound perfectly sensible. But in practice the promotion of industrial fishing, the lack of consistent policing, and the ludicrous 'quota' system, which forces fishermen to 'discard' millions of tonnes of fish a year dead back into the sea, have created one of the greatest man-made ecological disasters in the world.

The heart of the problem is that each of these policies exemplifies in acute form the central weakness which afflicts almost all the activities of our new 'European' form of government. By trying to impose labyrinthine bureaucratic structures on all the complexities of the real world, each has created a system which is in its own way no more workable than Stalin's Five Year Plans in the old USSR. Only the bureaucratic mind could devise a system which dictates precisely which types of fish a fishermen is permitted to catch, without realizing that, when he puts his net into the sea, it may well come up full of those for which Brussels has not given him a permit, and which therefore must be dumped back to pollute the ocean floor. Only the bureaucratic mind could devise a system which guarantees an intervention price to peach growers, without realizing this might result in EU taxpayers having to foot the bill for 650,000 tonnes of peaches to be bulldozed yearly into the ground.

The question is—what can be done? There has been talk of reforming the CAP for almost as long as anyone can remember. Yet whenever substantial changes have been made, like the McSharry reforms of 1992, these have only resulted in even more cost and bureaucracy than before. It would certainly be possible to devise policies both for farming and for fisheries which could produce infinitely greater social, economic, and environmental benefits than the present mess. But no one with the slightest knowledge of how the Brussels system works could imagine for a moment that any rational new policies are likely to emerge from that deadly combination of bureaucratic control-freakery and behind-the-scenes jockeying for national advantage.

And at this point one must face the inescapable fact that, for Britain, both the CAP and the CFP have brought an even greater disaster than anywhere else in the EU. The year when Britain's farm incomes reached their highest-ever level was 1973, the year we joined the CAP. Thirty years later British agriculture is going through its worst crisis in history, affecting every sector. Not all the reasons for this can be laid at the door of the CAP (BSE and collapsing world prices have been serious factors). But what is certain is that the CAP has done nothing whatever to help British farmers in this crisis. Indeed in many respects it has made it worse; not least because the British industry is in so many ways the Community's odd-man-out, and our government is now powerless to act independently to safeguard British interests even if it wished to.

Britain's only hope of achieving the fundamental reforms which might re-establish farming as a viable industry, based not least on its value in maintaining the countryside and in providing a wide range of the highest-quality food, from meat to specialist cheeses, would be through re-establishing national control over agriculture, so that farm policy could be reshaped to meet specific national needs. But this option is not on offer. The only conceivable alternative is that the collapse of British farming must continue, with all the social and environmental consequences that follow.

In fishing the disaster is caused by the simple fact that when something belongs to everyone, it belongs to no one. Again, it is perfectly possible to devise effective conservation policies, as has been shown in recent years by the examples of Canada, Norway, Iceland, and Namibia, all of which have managed dramatic stock recoveries through a combination of genuine science, modern technical measures, and strict enforcement. But this can only be done where a country takes responsibility for its own waters.

It is one of the real tragedies of recent British history that we should have been lulled into handing over the richest fishing waters in the world as part of our price for entering the Common Market in 1973. Had we not done so, the irony is that, under a proper conservation regime, continental fishermen could have continued to be given access to British waters on a bilateral basis, just as Norway allows EU vessels into her own waters now, and could have continued catching as many fish — but without the ecological disaster made inevitable under the obscenely wasteful system devised by Brussels. And, when this catastrophe is complete, it is one all Europe will have cause to regret.

WHY WE NEED THE CAP
Ben Gill

The Common Agricultural Policy has had a consistently bad press in the UK. Even those who are otherwise favourably inclined to the EU tend to dismiss it as at best an outdated failure.

In my view the critics have consistently missed the point: a Common Agricultural Policy has been and remains essential to the EU. This is not to say that the current policy is ideal; indeed it has already evolved considerably and will have to continue to do so in the future. But Europe without a common policy is neither a conceivable nor a desirable prospect.

A common myth trotted out about the CAP is that it represents some form of historic pact between the French and Germans. The French, so the story goes, were concerned in the 1950s that a common market in goods would expose their industry to the more competitive Germans and so, as a quid pro quo, they demanded an agricultural policy which would protect and subsidize, at German expense, their millions of peasant farmers. Like many myths, this seems plausible at first sight, but collapses as soon as it comes into contact with the facts. It was German agriculture which was less competitive (and largely remained so until reunification). It was the Germans who demanded and achieved a relatively high level of European agricultural subsidy from the outset of the EEC. The high guaranteed prices effectively protected German farmers, which both prevented a more thoroughgoing restructuring of farming and limited the extent to which French farmers were able to take advantage of the common market.

By obscuring the real reason for a common policy, this myth has contributed to the very serious misunderstanding of agricultural policy in this country. The truth is this: in the 1950s agriculture throughout Europe was a heavily subsidized industry, characterized by a large degree of government intervention. In the six founding EEC members the common system used was price support: in other words a guarantee to domestic farmers of a reasonable price level, achieved by import protection, public purchase of surpluses (intervention), and subsidies to allow exports outside Europe. In Britain, we subsidized farmers by direct top-up payments ('deficiency payments') to ensure farmers achieved an agreed price.

One of the primary aims (but certainly not the only aim, as many people in this country now like to pretend) of the EEC was to establish a common market for all goods, both industrial and agricultural. Now, in agriculture it would simply not have been possible to introduce free trade in a zone in which each country operated a very different level of price support; it would have led to huge economic distortions and would have been unacceptable to the farming population, which still constituted a significant part of the electorate. So it was necessary to have a common policy, where the level of subsidy was centrally decided, where rules were centrally enforced, and where the budgetary cost was shared.

Many commentators in the intervening years have speculated that if the UK had been part of the original EEC in 1958 a different kind of CAP would have emerged. Of course that may be true, and it may be that there would have been a system which relied more on direct subsidy to farmers. But there would still have been agricultural support. And there would still have had to be a Common Agricultural Policy, because it would have been equally unacceptable if the level of direct support to two identical farmers operating in two different countries within a common market were to be significantly different.

Forty years later, we are still in the same position. Agriculture is still an industry in which there is substantial government interference: this is the case not only in the EU but in the parts of Western Europe outside the EU (incidentally at a much higher level), in the USA, in Japan, and, with rare exceptions, in the whole of the industrialized world. So long as this situation continues, we need a common policy, not just in the interests of agriculture, but in the interests of the economy as a whole.

The original common market has now evolved into what has been since 1993 a 'single market', with no barriers whatsoever to trade and no customs posts or inspections. It follows that the single market is indivisible—you can't have it for some goods and not for others. Therefore, anything that threatens the free movement of goods in one sector threatens it in every sector. Going back to different national farming policies would very quickly threaten free trade.

Of course there are other possibilities, and it is right that we should examine them. One alternative would be for the UK to leave the CAP but remain within the EU's free trade area; another would be to imagine an evolution in which the whole of the EU renounces agricultural support, and the case for a common policy would fall.

First, the suggestion that the UK should leave the CAP but maintain free trade with the EU is often made, and occurs in a number of guises. In essence this is the 'Norway option': a supposed best-of-all-worlds whereby we keep free trade with the EU but avoid any damaging political entanglement.

An inconvenience of this suggestion is that in the case of Norway, Switzerland, Liechtenstein, and Iceland, free trade arrangements specifically exclude agriculture. That may be acceptable to those countries, which are not serious agricultural exporters, but would be no good for us. The EU is overwhelmingly our most important trading partner, accounting for approaching 80 per cent of our exports. And exports are a key to success, particularly in areas like sheep and cereals, where we export about a third of our production. So we need to stay in the single market.

The proposition thus comes down to saying that our farmers should be expected to compete with continental farmers, with a completely different level of public support. Let's take as an example the stated policy of the UK Independence Party. They say that outside the CAP we could have lower farm prices and lower subsidies: they suggest £2 billion a year (a substantial sum but about half what we currently receive). This is regarded as 'liberating' British agriculture: in my view as liberating as setting a lamb free amongst wolves. No industry in the UK would accept these terms of competition.

The second proposal, that the EU should renounce agricultural subsidies, needs to be taken more seriously. I have a number of observations to make, but perhaps the principal one is that we should recognize the extent to which the CAP is already evolving. As I have already mentioned, the CAP started out on the basis of supporting farmers' prices. That has already changed substantially, most notably in the 1992 reforms. In effect the EU has been forced to change the CAP in response to world concerns, expressed through the World Trade Organization, that high prices, import protection, and export subsidies are distorting world trade. The EU has therefore had to reduce prices and pay more and more support directly to farmers. The process continued in the 1999 CAP reform and it is a fair bet that future WTO negotiations will require further reforms.

A second pressure for change on the CAP has been the emergence of societal concerns. Fifty years ago the goal in

Britain and Europe was simple: to increase production. Now agricultural policy has to take account of all kinds of other, often competing objectives. We are no longer just looking at increasing production but at the needs of animal welfare, the environment, society, even cultural values. Agriculture has, in the inelegant jargon, become 'multifunctional'. Already the CAP is changing along these lines and now around 10 per cent of the total budget is spent on these types of measures. No doubt that share will increase in future.

There will also be pressure from future enlargement of the CAP to cover as many as 27 members. Often there is a glib assumption that enlargement will simply bring about the end of the CAP because the policy will become unaffordable. No doubt there will be serious financial pressures, but that is not the real point. The problem will be that the policy as it now stands is not in the true interests of many of the applicant countries. The economic logic is that they should receive much more from socio-economic measures and much less production support. But the political pressure, especially in Eastern European countries, is for them to be treated the same as us. I cannot predict how this conflict will be resolved, but there can be little doubt that it will cause a further shift in the CAP.

So the conclusion of my analysis is this. WTO pressures will require more support to be given in 'non-trade distorting' ways. In so far as this happens, this will in itself reduce the need for a centralized CAP, whose logic, as I have argued, is precisely that it is necessary to prevent trade distortion within Europe. Secondly, as more focus is placed on non-economic functions, like the environment and social issues, the more the logic for subsidiarity increases. Trade concerns require powerful European institutions to hold the ring; many environmental issues, for example, are often local or regional, and the need is for a targeted, not a centralized, approach. In my view enlargement will hasten this evolution.

I therefore foresee a gradual decline in the need for a centralized, monolithic CAP. But I emphasize this is a gradual evolution. What I do not see, and would not support, would be a 'big-bang' removal of all subsidies in Europe. I do not believe Europe can 'unilaterally disarm' in this way, unless all our major trading partners were to do the same. And, apart from anything else, the political will for this in the current EU simply does not exist.

IMPROVING THE POLICIES
Franz Fischler

The Common Agricultural Policy

The Common Agricultural Policy has had its fair share of criticism over the years, not least from concerned parties in the UK. Why should we have a common policy? Why do we even need a policy specifically for agriculture? These two questions—simple as they may seem—take us right to the heart of the debate.

When member states pooled forces to create a common policy for agriculture, they clearly recognized that substantial benefits would ensue. The free movement of agricultural goods provided for from the start under the CAP has clearly functioned as a trade booster, and the liberalization of agricultural trade flows has gradually increased the sector's competitiveness with the necessary adjustments in terms of internal common prices. But a common market needs common rules to ensure a level playing field—all the more so, in an increasingly integrated and enlarging Europe. In this regard, a single, non-discriminatory policy is clearly to be valued over 15 different agricultural policies, applied without any limitations.

This of course is no easy task—to set up a common policy, but one that takes account of the fact that agricultural systems and conditions of production differ among the diverse regions of the EU. Since its inception the CAP has been a policy delicately crafted to achieve a sensitive equilibrium between member states' interests. At the same time, it has to reconcile the multiple objectives set out in the Treaty of Rome—to increase productivity, to ensure a fair standard of living for farmers, to stabilize markets, to ensure the availability of supplies, and to ensure supplies reach consumers at reasonable prices.

While these objectives have remained fixed, the policy has constantly adapted to respond to the evolving demands and preoccupations of European society. Two substantial reforms over the past decade—most notably the historic Agenda 2000 reform—have equipped Europe's agricultural sector and rural economies to face the future. The reformed policy puts quality before quantity. It enhances the competitiveness of European farmers, enabling them to exploit the opportunities in domestic and world markets by producing high-value output in a way that is sound and environmentally friendly. To this end, the new CAP provides for strict food quality and safety rules. This is all the more important as we have all been living with the consequences of BSE and continue to do so. Public confidence in food safety, in the national administrations, in the CAP, and beyond this in the European integration process itself has been severely shocked.

It should, however, be said that it was not the EU which forced farmers to feed meat and bonemeal to cattle. On the contrary, as long ago as 1994 the European Commission took measures to ban meat and bonemeal from ruminant feed. Furthermore, the EU has adopted a framework of measures and a battery of controls, provided by legislation, to tackle BSE, and if these controls are respected and implemented, the risk to the public is reduced to a minimum. Of course these controls can only be effective if properly implemented. However many controls are built into a system, the correct application will always depend on the goodwill of individuals. Doing the right thing cannot only be imposed by legislation and control systems. To some extent it is also a matter of ethics.

Today, however, agriculture provides many services to society beyond the essential function of food production. Protecting the environment, enriching our rural heritage, and maintaining a vibrant rural sector feature among these services. To safeguard these public services, agricultural policy should guide farmers to provide them. Sustaining the livelihood of farmers while promoting the sustainable development of the wider rural economy is therefore a key driving force of the new CAP.

The evidence lies in our new policy for rural development. This policy supports investment in agricultural holdings, young farmers, and those in less favoured areas, to name but a few priorities. With a view to widening the economic fabric in rural areas, diversification is encouraged. To promote sustainability, protection of the environment is brought to the fore, with agri-environment schemes constituting the only compulsory element of member states' rural development programmes. These schemes allow for member states to make direct payments conditional on environmentally sound farming practices.

The CAP, however, is not a straitjacket that offers no freedom of movement, for it is built increasingly on the principles of decentralization. Taking the example of rural development, the policy has been designed to be flexible and can be tailored to regional and local needs. A further example of the flexibility offered under the CAP is the modulation principle, which gives member states the possibility to reduce direct payments for large farms and to use them for additional rural development measures. The UK was one of the first member states to take up this option.

All these elements that make up the new CAP are evidence of a policy that is comprehensive and multi-faceted, capable of responding to the opportunities and challenges of the new millennium within the 15 EU member states and eventually beyond once enlargement has taken place.

The need for a better Common Fisheries Policy

The dramatic reductions in the total allowable catches for cod and other important fish species decided by the Council of Ministers last year have once more put the Common Fisheries Policy under the spotlight in the UK. For critics of the CFP, the continued depletion of fish stocks demonstrates the failure of the policy. They advocate repatriating fisheries management, arguing that the UK would make a better job of managing fisheries in its waters. While accepting that substantial improvements of today's CFP are required, I believe that it is the only realistic way to manage European fisheries, for three reasons.

First, given the highly mobile nature of fish and fishing, the EU needs a common fisheries policy. Fish stocks move across international borders; most of them are fished in more than one member state and by more than one fishing fleet. International negotiations and international cooperation are intrinsic to fisheries management in Europe. Even in the absence of a CFP, the member states would still have to come to an understanding between themselves and with third countries, such as Norway or the Baltic states, about these common resources. The problems would be exactly the same: to agree on a common strategy for exploiting fish stocks, to share fishing rights, to reduce conflict between different types of fishing, and to ensure fair and effective enforcement of common rules. None of those problems would be any easier to solve outside the current Community framework.

Second, quite apart from the inevitability of international cooperation, the CFP provides significant added value to what could be achieved through the individual efforts of member states. Through this means the Community mobilizes significant human and financial resources for scientific research, the collection of data, structural aid to help the fisheries sector adjust to change, and international cooperation. The Community speaks with a single voice in all its external fisheries relations, whether in its dealings with neighbouring coastal states or with regional and international fisheries organizations around the globe.

A third reason for the CFP is that the links between fisheries and other policy areas in which the need for Community-level action is undisputed (such as environmental policy, health and consumer protection, maintenance of the single market, or development or competition policy) mean that even if the CFP did not yet exist the Community would have to invent it. Only 'joined-up' policy-making at Community level can provide an adequate response to the key questions we are facing in these fields, such as the protection of marine mammals or birds, prevention of pollution of fishing grounds, the gradual elimination of dioxin or heavy metals in fish, extending our relationship with developing countries, or action against irresponsible fishing using flags of convenience.

The Union still faces major policy challenges in the fisheries field, however, which need to be addressed urgently.

The main one is over-capacity of the fishing fleet, which, aided and abetted over the years by subsidies, is the main cause of stock depletion. Fish are now paying the price of measures which have not gone far enough to ensure a better balance between the number, size, and power of fishing vessels and available resources. Only a smaller fishing industry than the one we have today is sustainable both in economic and biological terms. EU aid is available to help affected fishing communities diversify their economies.

Another challenge is to increase the involvement of fishing communities in the decision-making process. We are already heading in this direction but we need to go further. Member states are already responsible for the management of fisheries within the 12-mile band round their coasts. In the UK, producers' organizations manage catch quotas. Regional workshops on specific fisheries bring together representatives of the fishermen and the administrations concerned with the scientists to look at the best ways to manage these fisheries. However, more can and must be done to increase the involvement of interested parties and to harness local expertise.

The CFP will also have to tackle the problem of waste. Fishermen discard fish when they have no quotas for their catches, or when fish is under the minimum landing size, or when they wish to retain the most valuable fish for the market. In Community waters most fisheries are 'mixed', making it very difficult for fishermen not to catch other species along with those they target. There is no easy solution to this problem. Allowing the landing of all fish caught might reduce the levels of discards, but it may also encourage fishermen to disregard their quotas and deliberately target young fish. However, the Commission is ready to propose various measures, including the possibility of setting up pilot projects for discard management in specific fisheries with the prior agreement of the fishermen concerned.

The Commission will this year open a major political debate on how to improve the CFP. A number of elements of the policy have to be reviewed in 2002 and the Commission has taken this opportunity to examine what needs to be changed. The UK Fishermen's Federations have already submitted constructive suggestions and I would invite all other interested parties to contribute to the debate. Our objective is clear—to ensure sustainable fisheries in the EU.

7 THE ENVIRONMENT

The EU has passed hundreds of specific anti-pollution measures, and its role in environmental protection tends to have greater public backing than any other area. But questions also arise about the environmental impact of its wider policies and the principles by which it should operate.

COMMON EUROPEAN ACTION

John Gummer

There can be no effective national environmental policy in the UK. Only a policy rooted in common European action can meet our national needs. That understanding is widely shared even among those who are much more sceptical about other areas of EU activity. Opinion polls consistently show strong support in the UK and across Europe for the EU's role in the environment. The facts back that up. Half of the air pollution we suffer in Britain derives from the continent, and we export to them half of what we produce here. Our attempts to clean up the seas around us would be doomed if the Elbe and the Rhine were to continue to pollute. Even in narrower interest fields this interdependence is increasingly obvious. The million members of the Royal Society for the Protection of Birds know how important to our bird life are migrant species and therefore how interested we should be in the protection of continental habitats and the effective control of the shooting of wild birds.

So, too, in the increasingly internationalized commercial and manufacturing world, environmental standards cannot be nationally based. There isn't a popular motor car that is made entirely in Britain. With an engine from Germany, transmission from Spain, Italian fittings, and French tyres, it would be impossible to control on a national basis the noise, emissions, energy content, and recyclability—even of what's left. European directives on vehicles and their 'end of life', on tyres and their disposal, on emissions and their reduction—these are essential elements in a wider environmental regime.

Of course, the biggest driving force for that regime will be the urgency of combating climate change. Europe has already shown itself the leader in this response. The EU 'bubble', in which the richer member nations do more so that the poorer may do less, will be seen as a model for much wider implementation. Setting the pace will inevitably lead to clashes with the US, where the appreciation of the issue is culturally much more difficult. Pushing forward from the Kyoto conference on climate change will be hard, but the strength of the EU is sufficient to make it possible. Alone, none of us would be strong enough. Only the growing unity in Europe saves us from the disaster that unchallenged American attitudes would produce.

Europe will phase out the use of HFCs—the greenhouse gases used in refrigeration and air conditioning—even before there is a worldwide ban. Tough energy efficiency rules for manufactured goods may well invite US antagonism. Even more certainly, American refusal to reduce emissions will increase tensions as it becomes clear that

this failure is changing the climate of us all. A clearer invasion of sovereignty it would be difficult to imagine — 4 per
cent of the world's population producing 25 per cent of the
world's emissions and changing the climate of 100 per
cent of the world's nation-states. In changing this, Europe
will have to forge alliances with the third world — particularly India and China — to insist on a global answer to this
truly global problem. It is only by regional strength that we
shall force the pace sufficiently to reach cooperative decisions in time.

In the free world we shall need to use market mechanisms to achieve our environmental ends and create a
sustainable society. Yet, in Europe, we are only at the
beginning in using regulatory measures to make the market reflect the true cost of what we buy. The market is better at representing present cost than recognizing future
liabilities. For generations we have taken profits based on
the calculation of our immediate outlay and left the
clean-up to the future. Private transactions rarely take
proper account of the cost to the public purse, either
immediately or in the long run.

So tyre manufacturers have been able to sell their products
without shouldering the responsibility and cost of hand-
ling the tyre once it is worn out. Fields, rivers, ponds, and
smoking pyres increasingly evidence the problem, yet the
makers still argue that someone else should pay.

Again, no national solution will suffice and the EU will
have to produce a framework within which manufacturers
and retailers properly share those real costs that have not

so far been reflected in the price. Tyres and batteries, packaging and white goods, vehicles and electronic equipment—the pricing of all the material products of modern life needs to reflect the larger cost. For years we have recognized the need to account for depreciation but our definition has been too limited. A society that intends to be sustainable cannot so limit depreciation that it applies only to the process of making and selling. The cost cycle must be completed to include consuming. Only in that way do we not leave bills to others, while we take the profits for ourselves. All liabilities must be reflected in the price, although competition demands that that reflection must not distort the single market. The framework therefore needs to be European. At the same time, cost-effectiveness requires that the mechanisms be as market-oriented and as locally sensitive as possible.

Together that argues for a firm framework within which business achieves these environmental ends in the cheapest possible way. Here, national schemes within a European regime ought to compete one with another as long as they meet increasingly rigorous targets set by the EU. Already in packaging recovery, reuse, and recycling, the UK will meet its targets at a cost hugely below that demanded by the bureaucratic German system. This competitive advantage can only be good as it delivers sustainability at the least possible cost, ensures that the process is market driven, and removes environmental action from stifling bureaucratic restriction. Over the next couple of decades, European industry will come to accept a pricing regime that internalizes its real costs in almost every area.

Yet merely picking up the tab for costs incurred will not be enough. There is much to be done to drive eco-efficiency within the Union. We shall see clearer and more universal labelling of products to improve consumer choice. We shall see too a significant raising of minimum standards.

Dishwashers and washing machines will use less water and more friendly detergent. Standby systems, with their little red eyes in the corner of every sitting room, will give way to mechanisms that do not use such a huge amount of power. Energy efficiency will increase dramatically in white goods and vehicles, in computers, air conditioning, and refrigeration. All this will be driven by European voluntary agreements backed up by minimum standards, akin to our building regulations. The battle will be to ensure that these are not prescriptive but instead set tough standards and leave it to industry to find the best way to conform. This kind of regulation encourages innovation. Prescription stultifies change.

At the same time Europe will need to help to turn globalization into something more than compulsory free trade. The riches that are promised from a global market cannot be achieved without global responsibility. Free trade is good but it is not the only good. There is much in the depth of European civilization, not least in the tradition of Christian Democracy, which understands that more completely than does the New World. The outburst at Seattle should be a warning to us all. We cannot create global free trade without the proper protections that we demand in our own nation-states. Just as we insist that we take account, at home, of the vulnerability of people and of the environment, so too we must act on the global scale. It is Europe's task to bring the values of the Old World to the rescue of the New.

In all this Britain has a pivotal role. Our commitment to the market is crucial if environmental concern is not to become the excuse for centralized control and bureaucratic regulation. Our understanding of the virtues of competition must guide Europe away from prescription and restriction.

Yet Britain's position is not in doubt, only its engagement. We have been semi-detached for far too long. The only thing that can stop us from fulfilling our historic role is our own unwillingness to be involved. Our self-image stands in the way of acting effectively in our own interests. We are so frightened of domination that we dare not give an inch in Europe even if it is to gain a mile. Some would even prefer to be the agents of America than the partners of Europe. They would happily surrender to the US a sovereignty they will not even share with those with whom by geography, culture, religion, and history Britain is indissolubly linked.

Yet it is not a choice between the US and Europe. Britain brings to Europe what is best in thrusting capitalism, and it takes from our common heritage the values that go far beyond it. It is that respect for the past and responsibility for the future that underlies our growing commitment to sustainability. Together we Europeans can be the equal allies and friends of the US and in that equality we shall find a mutual respect that uncritical acceptance and unequal domination could never achieve.

EUROPE'S ANTI-ENVIRONMENTAL DRIFT

Stephen Tindale

Most of the environmental laws in force in the UK today started life in Brussels. Improvements in air and water quality, statutory protection for important wildlife habitats, reductions in pollution from cars and incinerators have all come as a result of European directives. It would be easy to conclude that the EU is a force for environmental progress, and that greater integration is a prerequisite for sustainable salvation. Easy, but wrong.

Closer European union does not automatically protect the natural world. Britain has higher environmental standards as an EU member than it would have done if we had remained outside, but this is simply a reflection of the low priority given to the environment by successive British governments. Norway has shown that a nation-state with a high environmental consciousness can implement strong policies without being an EU member. Indeed, the fear that EU membership would weaken environmental protection was one of the key factors in the Norwegian public's decision not to join.

It is a truism that pollution does not respect national boundaries. Norway's impressive range of environmental policies does not prevent acid gases from British power stations damaging Norwegian lakes. Environmental problems cannot be solved by individual governments acting alone. But this does not mean that the entire panoply of EU institutions, policies, and doctrines is needed. Much of the progress on combating air pollution in Europe has come in an inter-governmental forum, the UN Economic Commission for Europe.

The environment was not part of the original Treaty of Rome. Jean Monnet's dream of a Common Market was based on free trade. The Coal and Steel Community was based on producer protection. The Euratom Treaty was based on the false promise of cheap, safe nuclear power. Europe's approach to the environment has been to graft environmental protection on to existing, generally damaging policies. This has led to 'end of pipe' solutions rather than the promotion of cleaner, more efficient patterns of production: filters on power stations, for example, rather than energy systems delivering power efficiently from renewable sources. Or attempts to preserve small islands of wildlife value amid the general picture of subsidized destruction.

On balance, EU membership has been good for the British environment. But it is not clear that in future the EU will be a positive force. To ensure that it is, the EU needs more than the institutional tinkering discussed but not agreed at Nice, such as more qualified majority voting on environmental matters. It needs a fundamental reassessment of how the environment fits into the European project.

Completion of the single market has become the central obsession of EU policy-makers. Anything which might impede the free movement of goods and services is dismissed as wicked, whatever its other merits. This drive to remove every barrier to trade is the most centralizing process imaginable—a fact conveniently overlooked by Thatcherites condemning Brussels 'meddling'. In the name of the single market, member states have lost their right to protect their citizens and their environments. Protection is entrusted instead to the EU, and far too often the EU has erred on the side of producer rather than consumer interests, leaving European citizens dangerously exposed.

Trade rules dictate that national governments should not ban things without good reason. The rules of the World Trade Organization define the exemptions—areas where countries can legitimately restrict trade—fairly broadly, including the need to protect human health, plants, and animals. European law is more restrictive. It lays down detailed procedures for making decisions and then makes it all but impossible for member states to depart from these decisions.

Sadly, the procedures are not robust. The burden of proof is placed on those wishing to demonstrate a problem, rather than those claiming that a product or process is safe. EU chemicals policy is the starkest example. New chemicals have to undergo toxicity tests; not as stringent as they should be, but better than nothing. Nothing is precisely what manufacturers of existing chemicals, those which were on the market before the EU regulation came into force, need to do. Yet only 7 per cent of the chemicals in common household products have undergone adequate toxicity testing, according to the British Medical Association. That means that for 93 per cent of common household chemicals we do not know what they are doing to us and our children.

The EU approach to this scandal has been to concoct systems so byzantine that only a handful of chemicals have been assessed over the last two decades. Unless there is incontrovertible proof of harm, the need to keep chemicals flowing freely around Europe is deemed more important than the need to protect people. EU chemicals policy is currently being reviewed, and the Swedish presidency has made it a priority. This review needs to reverse the policy: in future, chemicals should only be sold if their effects are understood.

Policy on genetically modified organisms is similarly lax. Products do have a number of regulatory hurdles to clear, but these look at whether any evidence of possible harm exists, not whether the existing evidence is sufficient to ensure safety. Insufficient knowledge is not deemed a legitimate reason for member states to block products. They can only opt out of an EU decision if they can show new evidence. If there is no data, there is no evidence of harm; therefore the products are deemed safe.

No one has ever asked Europe's citizens whether they value the notional benefits of single market completion — essentially an extra few percentage points of economic growth — more highly than their own protection or the preservation of their environment. The enthusiasm for ever freer trade is undermining the Western European social market model and so destroying the political basis for European integration.

If the single market programme is environmentally dangerous, the Common Agricultural Policy has been an unmitigated disaster. There is not space here to analyse the shortcomings of the CAP, nor is it really necessary. Its failings are widely perceived and distressingly visible. The sensible solution is also broadly agreed: a move away from price support towards income support for individual small farmers, coupled with payments to all farmers to ensure that they preserve the landscape, promote wildlife diversity, and produce healthy food.

The problem has always been to get sensible change through an Agriculture Council on which the reactionary elements of German and French farming have an apparent stranglehold. But the spread of BSE throughout Europe has left the intensive farming lobby on the defensive. German Chancellor Schröder has thrown his weight behind a move to organic and extensive production. Britain has always said that it favours fundamental reform of the CAP; now is its chance to seize the opportunity to lead an alliance for change.

Farmland wildlife is in steep decline, but even that looks healthy compared to the state of Europe's fish stocks. The Common Fisheries Policy has succeeded in driving fish which were once common to the edge of commercial extinction. Again Britain is broadly on the side of reform. The fisheries minister, Elliot Morley, has done well arguing for change, but this needs to be elevated to higher levels of government. As a maritime nation, the UK should argue that preservation of the environmental and economic health of the seas is part of our vital national interest.

A reassessment of the single market project; overhaul of the CAP and CFP: these are things which must be done to correct the anti-environmental drift of European integration. Is there anything more positive, a project which could make environmentalists more than reluctant Europeans?

The answer is that the EU could be used to deliver a transformation of European economies away from fossil fuels and nuclear power to renewable energy. People who have not researched the subject often assume that renewables will always be marginal.

Yet a combination of wind power, solar photovoltaics, biomass, and small-scale hydro power could meet all of our energy needs. Power from intermittent sources can be stored as hydrogen, for use to power fuel cells in both stationary plants and vehicles.

The EU needs to transform its energy systems in the next two decades in the way agriculture was transformed in the first 20 years of integration, but this time with the environment as a central concern. To achieve this, the continuing pro-nuclear bias in EU institutions, a hangover from Euratom days, needs to be eradicated. The liberalization of energy markets needs to be fashioned in a way which enables governments to promote efficiency and renewable generation. If these goals conflict, liberalization should give way.

Europe is a densely populated, intensively farmed continent. Neglecting the environment and promoting destructive industrial and agricultural policies has a severe impact not only on nature, but also on people. If European integration is to win over sceptical public opinion, in the UK and elsewhere, it needs to offer more than economic functionalism. It needs to offer a European home that people want to live in.

8 THE SOCIAL AGENDA

This has often been a matter of contention between Britain and most other EU countries. The most dramatic illustration of this was the Maastricht summit in 1991, when John Major secured the British opt-out on the 'Social Chapter' of the treaty under negotiation. It covered issues like working hours, parental leave, and benefits for part-time workers. The other 11 countries were forced to relegate these provisions from the main body of the treaty to a protocol, which they all agreed to while Britain did not. Similarly in 1989, when Margaret Thatcher was prime minister, the British government had alone stood out against the Social Charter, which proclaimed greater rights for employees.

While the Blair government signed the Social Chapter soon after its election in 1997, there is still an underlying philosophical difference between the British approach of favouring more flexible labour markets and a stress on promoting enterprise, as against the continental social protection model, with its regulatory emphasis and much consensual talk of social partners (employers and unions). However, these differences are currently tending to narrow as on both sides there has been some movement towards the middle.

STANDING UP TO THE MULTINATIONALS
John Monks

The technical foundations for EU enlargement were set in
Nice, but the 'big issues' about the future of the EU have
been put back until 2004, the date envisaged for the next
Inter-Governmental Conference. The agreement that
there will be wide-ranging discussions with all interested
parties is welcome. The trade union movement will of
course take part in them, arguing in particular that fundamental economic and social rights such as those set down
in the charter proclaimed in Nice are intrinsic to the
Union's fabric.

Sovereignty-related issues should be clearly and openly
engaged in the coming debate. The eurosceptic right are
on the whole happy with the EU as an instrument for free-
ing up markets. Yet they denounce the delivery mechanisms; Baroness Thatcher has recanted over one of her
greater achievements in Europe—signing up to the Single
European Act. They will not countenance the idea that
markets have social and political dimensions, yet
the moral rectitude of free markets figures high in their

thinking. They have nothing to say about the real democratic deficit that is emerging in this globalized world.

The real source of power is the increasingly mighty multinational corporation. Of the 100 largest economies in the world, only half are countries. In 2000 the market capitalization of Microsoft overtook the GNP of a G7 country—Canada. General Motors is worth two Denmarks. Nokia is valued at more than twice the value of its home state, Finland. Apart from the US, if it had the inclination, no country on earth has the countervailing weight to stand up to multinationals. But the EU is now the world's largest single market. It can and does set standards for the EU area which can also impact worldwide.

The eurosceptic right chooses to see little wrong with making the world open territory for multinationals. Indeed they reserve their biggest fire for any European measures that do rein them in, such as moves to increase the rights of their employees or to protect the environment. They much prefer the US model, where big corporate money dominates the political process—and incidentally half the population don't vote.

Nation-states the size of the UK need to pool aspects of their sovereignty if they are actually going to have any sovereignty at all. It has been true in the defence of the West, and it is equally true when it comes to taming these enormously powerful new world powers which play to the rules of enhancing shareholder value, often it seems with no other priority in mind. The UK in the EU has a chance to exert a decisive influence, the UK on its own virtually none.

The regulation of international trade is much more than a technical issue. Essential national interests are involved, as any look at current disputes between the US and the EU before the World Trade Organization will demonstrate. In this respect the EU acts as one, represented by the Commission with a mandate agreed by the Council. It is generally accepted that having Leon Brittan or Pascal Lamy as the trade commissioner negotiating for all results in preferable outcomes for France or the UK to those they would have obtained acting alone. The WTO example makes a general point. We need some political catch-up to match the economic reality.

The EU will develop in its own way. The trend in Nice was, to coin a phrase, towards a third way, leaning towards inter-governmentalism and away from the community method. The seeds of this approach can be found in the Employment Title introduced in the Amsterdam Treaty. This has brought the European Council into play in quite detailed policy-making, first in Luxembourg and then in Lisbon, to modernize Europe's economic and social approaches. The European Council is a relatively recent institution in Treaty terms, and is inherently an inter-governmental body.

This has engendered new approaches and processes, embedded for example in the European Social Agenda adopted in Nice. The so-called 'open coordination' method, involving guidelines, benchmarking, and targets, for example, and bringing the social partners into the process, has become a useful adjunct to the traditional legislative means. But these should not be discounted. According to the polls, people like what Europe has delivered on the social front. Indeed the government should avoid the seductive temptation to claim for itself credit for good things that come from Europe. For example, it is thanks to Europe that UK workers are no longer the only group without a legal right to paid holidays anywhere in the EU.

In addition, and it is a matter of horses for courses, we have the procedures involving the social partners introduced in the Maastricht social protocol and integrated in the Amsterdam Treaty. These procedures, which have given us, for example, parental leave provisions and rights for part-time workers, make it possible for the social partners to reach framework agreements that leave it for the nations to fill in the details by way of national regulation and other arrangements. National implementation itself can, and should, be done through social partner involvement. This affords flexibility and subsidiarity.

Enhanced cooperation is another form of flexibility. The British government rightly opposes the creation of a hard core, in which some member states create their own set of shared policies and institutions from which the others are in practice excluded. That objective was formally protected in Nice. But the reality test revolves around Economic and Monetary Union—which of course forms the backdrop to any discussion about Europe in Britain.

It would be wrong to believe that remaining on the sideline of EMU would not result in second-class membership. In addition to strictly defined euro issues, including dialogue with the European Central Bank, the euro group of nations will be discussing further coordination of economic policies, in particular in the context of structural reforms, for example, concerning pensions and employment. The group will increasingly become the focus for EU governance while — as Chris Patten described it graphically — British diplomats hover outside the meeting room and pick up what scraps they can about plans for economic and monetary policy, but have no say.

If there is a silver lining to George W Bush's capture of the White House, it is that we might hear a little less here about the shining example that the US can offer Europe in its economic and social policies, and a little more about the advantages which full participation in the EU, including EMU, can bring to Britain.

Of course, no one could have advocated entering the euro at the typical exchange rates of last year. But this is now changing. There is still some way to go before we achieve a fully competitive pound, but the movement is now in the right direction for the UK to pass this key test from the trade union point of view. If it is clear that the economic conditions are right, that the chancellor's five tests would be met, and yet there is still no action, then we run a huge risk. If the world's boardrooms decide British membership of the euro has shifted from being a question of 'when' to one of 'whether', we will start to pay a much greater price.

There is a danger that more multinational and British companies would say that they cannot run the risks of continuing exchange rate instability between the currency in which they pay their costs and the currency in which they get paid. So the campaign about entry must be engaged. This should be an integral part of the prepare side of the 'prepare and decide' equation. It is not simply a technical question.

RED TAPE KILLS ENTERPRISE

Ruth Lea

When the UK joined the European Community in 1973 the British public were led to believe that it would be little more than joining a free trade area. Alas, they were misled. This never was the case, as official papers recently released (under the 30-year rule) clearly show. And now, some 28 years later, the EU has enormous influence and power on British law and institutions. Employment law and businesses are no exceptions.

Before looking at specific legislation, I would like to outline briefly how we have arrived at this position. To start at the very beginning, the Treaty of Rome in 1957 included references to social policies (including labour law and industrial relations). It also touched on the concept of the 'harmonization' of working conditions, as well as standards of living and social systems. The Commission adopted its first Social Action Programme in 1974, which included provisions concerning the improvement and upward harmonization of working conditions. Several similar programmes which attempted to widen the regulation of employment practices followed this.

171

The Single European Act (SEA) in 1986 provided the next major boost for social harmonization. It included initiatives for extending the regulation of employment practices and permitted qualified majority voting for health and safety directives. The Social Charter (Community Charter of Fundamental Social Rights for Workers), which was a declaration of principle rather than a legislative programme, followed the SEA. It was adopted in 1989 by 11 of the 12 EC countries (the UK dissenting) and emphasized new employee 'rights' and 'freedoms'. In the wake of the Charter, the Commission set in hand a five-year Social Action Programme (1990–5) to implement the Charter throughout the EC.

The next stage along the road to social harmonization was the Protocol on Social Policy and Agreement on Social Policy (the 'Social Chapter'), which was appended to the Treaty on European Union. The 'Social Chapter' had originally been intended as part of the Treaty but was taken out because of the UK's refusal to agree to yet another boost to yet more EU social regulation. But the new Labour government agreed to end Britain's Social Chapter 'opt-out' at the Amsterdam Summit in 1997, and a single framework for social policy (covering all members of the EU) was included in the Treaty of Amsterdam.

The Social Policy Agenda (SPA) was agreed at the Nice summit last December. Rather like the Social Charter, this is not a legislative programme as such, but lays out a wide range of objectives including strengthening gender equality, improving social protection, and combating discrimination. These are of course noble aspirations, but more legislation is sure to follow. And the added legislation can only hinder rather than help the progress of some of the SPA's other main objectives—specifically, to encourage dynamic entrepreneurial behaviour and to exploit the potential of the knowledge-based economy. More red tape and the encouragement of enterprise are, I suggest, totally incompatible.

And finally, the interpretation of employment law by the European Court of Justice will be influenced by the Charter of Fundamental Human Rights of the EU, which includes the 'right to strike'. This Charter was also agreed at Nice.

With so many initiatives, rights, and freedoms for workers, British employers may well wonder when the EU will ever consider their rights and treatment in the workplace!

'Harmonization' and the consequences of heavy regulation

EU social harmonization policies are intended to 'create a level playing field' and to prevent 'social dumping' and 'unfair labour market competition', but they are more likely to restrict any competition, however fair or unfair. The directives aimed at 'harmonization' are, moreover, disproportionately damaging for the UK's competitive position because of our relatively lightly regulated labour markets (or at least they were, but our competitive advantage in this respect has certainly been eroded over the past three years). But EU labour market harmonization does not just damage British competitiveness vis-à-vis the rest of the EU; it damages it with the rest of the world. The British economy is global.

Labour market regulations in the EU's continental economies are hugely onerous (with the possible exceptions of the Netherlands and Denmark) and, along with the high social on-costs, undoubtedly discourage job creation. Unemployment rates in France, Germany, and Italy are still around 9–10 per cent compared with 5.5 per cent in the UK (on the International Labour Organization definition). Moreover, the labour force participation rates are lower in continental Europe's 'big three' countries than in the UK. Germany's participation rate is around 74.5 per cent, whilst the French and Italian rates are 68 per cent and under 60 per cent respectively. In the UK it is 76 per cent.

The tragedy of labour market regulations (many of which are intended to improve job security and 'protect' people's jobs) is that they are often counterproductive. Regulations destroy jobs rather than create and 'protect' them. I believe strongly that the EU's social policy should be determined by reference to economic competitiveness rather than the outdated concept of labour market protectionism. And even though many of the EU's social policies are couched in terms of 'fairness', there can be little 'fair' about pricing people out of work by increasing work-related regulations on employers.

The extent of the EU's employment legislation

There is no doubt that the impact of the EU on employment law is considerable and growing. In some areas of human resources (HR) practice EU policy is dominant. And, as successive EU employment directives have been adopted at EU level and then 'very thoroughly' implemented into UK law, businesses (and their HR departments if they have one) have had to introduce significant change to existing HR custom and practice in almost all cases.

A table of selected directives appears at the end of this text—it is far from being comprehensive. According to the Chartered Institute of Personnel and Development there have been to date over 50 directives that have been adopted in the field of social and employment policy. As can be seen from the table, EU influence on nearly all areas of the employment relationship has grown dramatically since the mid-1990s.

Moreover, as can also be seen from the table, the range and extent of EU-originating legislation is considerable. It can broadly be classified into four groups. The first group is extensive and relates to equal opportunities. It includes the Equal Pay, the Parental Leave, and the anti-discrimination Directives. (As a result of the Treaty of Amsterdam new competencies were created in the areas of race-, age-, disability-, and sexual orientation-discrimination legislation.) Apart from the general increase in regulations, there has been a very disturbing development in the recent anti-discrimination directives. In all three (sex, race, and the 'General Framework') the reversal of the burden of proof will operate. If a case is brought against an employer, he/she will have to prove his/her innocence. This is grotesquely unfair.

The second group, also extensive, relates to employment protection and working conditions and includes collective redundancies, part-time work, fixed term work, and temporary work. The third group includes the very bureaucratic Working Time Directive and general health and safety at work directives. The final group covers employee consultation and comprises the European Works Councils and the proposed Information and Consultation of Workers Directive. Both of these directives could severely impair the ability of business to make speedy competitiveness-sustaining and -enhancing decisions. And moreover they are quite alien to British business custom.

Impact on British business: red tape kills enterprise

The evidence is there for all to see. The impact on British business of EU employment law is very considerable. But, alas, there is absolutely no sign of EU 'initiative fatigue'. Not only do new treaties such as Maastricht and Amsterdam introduce new areas of competency within which the EU can legislate, but the EU process itself creates a steady stream of legislative action requiring implementation at member-state level. The tide shows no sign of being reversed and with each initiative and each directive there comes more red tape. It is red tape which can only distract businesspeople from running their businesses properly, creating wealth and jobs. 'Small' businesspeople find the never-ending avalanche of regulations particularly irksome as they struggle with the paperwork. Red tape kills enterprise.

And, as I have already said, many labour market regulations are based on the old-fashioned notion of protection, stifle job creation, and are quite counterproductive. I cannot believe that any politician here or in the rest of the EU really wishes this to happen. And yet it does. EU social and labour policies need a radical rethink. The EU needs to stop meddling with business and let businesspeople get on with running their businesses and, yes, creating jobs.

Selected directives relating to social and employment issues

1975	Equal Pay Directive
1975	Collective Redundancies Directive
1976	Equal Treatment Directive (several daughter directives followed)
1977	Transfers of Undertakings (Protection of Employment) Directive (TUPE) or Acquired (Employee) Rights Directive
1980	Insolvencies Directive
1989	Health and Safety Framework Directive (several daughter directives followed)
1991	Proof of Employment Relationship Contract
1991	Temporary Workers Directive

1992	Protection of Pregnant Women at Work Directive
1993	Working Time Directive
1994	European Works Councils Directive
1996	Parental Leave Directive
1996	Posting of Workers Directive
1997	Burden of Proof in Sex Discrimination Cases Directive
1997	Amsterdam Summit: the UK signs the Social Chapter
1998	Part-time Workers Directive
1999	Fixed Term Work Directive
2000	Equal Treatment (Racial or Ethnic Origin) Directive
2000	General Framework for the Equal Treatment in Employment and Occupation Directive
Under discussion	Information and Consultation of Workers Directive

9 INTERNAL DEMOCRACY

For years talk of the 'democratic deficit' within the EU has been commonplace. Its institutions suffer from a lack of democratic accountability, legitimacy, and popularity. Attempts to tackle this over the past decade have led to a substantial increase in powers for the European Parliament, the one directly elected part of the EU system. But few people are satisfied that this has dealt with the problem.

If the diagnosis is commonplace, the remedy is a matter of great dispute. For some people the solution is to take the process of empowering the European Parliament much further. Others believe that the institutions within the EU which possess the most democratic legitimacy are the elected governments of member states, and so that the way forward is an increase in 'inter-governmentalism', based on direct dealings between governments, with a smaller role for the Commission (this is the approach underlying Tony Blair's Warsaw speech). On the other hand there are those for whom any attempt to build a cross-national European democracy is fraught with danger and probably doomed to failure. Meanwhile, there are some who seek to transcend this debate with more radical and innovative solutions.

THE CASE FOR A FEDERAL EUROPE

John Pinder

Clarity is needed about a concept that has been so much abused in British politics. A federal polity is simply one with democratic government at two or more levels, where states give powers to a federal government to deal with their common affairs but retain those that concern their internal affairs. The institutions at both levels are based on representative government, the rule of law, and citizens' rights, with the division of powers between the states and the union constitutionally guaranteed. This essay argues that the British interest lies in a European Union with a democratic federal government.

This builds on what exists. The Union has already moved quite far in a federal direction. Its institutions have been able to shoulder its responsibilities in the economy and the environment precisely because of the steps taken to give them federal elements at intervals during the past half-century. The cynical description of the process as a slippery slope is the opposite of the truth. Each step has been hard to take, but agreed by the member states to enable the Union to provide benefits for the citizens that they cannot provide separately.

The EU and its pre-federal institutions

The rule of law is fundamental in the EU. The Court of Justice has ensured that the law of the European Community, which is the heart of the EU, is observed. The result has been a shift from power-based to law-based relations between the several states, across the broad range of Community competences: a major contribution to making war between them unthinkable.

The legislature of the EU, like that of a federation, comprises a house of the states and a house of the citizens, responsible for enacting the laws and controlling the Commission. The directly elected European Parliament is halfway towards having the powers of a federal house of the citizens: it co-decides, with the Council of Ministers, over half of the legislation and the budget; and it was the Parliament, not the Council, that used its powers to secure the resignation of the Commission in March 1999. But instead of conveying a clear message to the citizens that laws are enacted and the budget approved by both the Parliament and the Council, the system is a maze of complicated procedures; and instead of explaining to the public the importance of the Parliament to European democracy, political leaders tend to ignore or disparage it.

The Council of Ministers is closer to having the powers of a federal house of the states, but, unlike any democratic legislature, it enacts the legislation behind closed doors and is still distinguished by the fairly extensive scope for the veto. It also retains executive powers not proper to a legislature, without being accountable to any other institution for that part of its work: a concentration of legislative and executive powers that flouts the principles of liberal democracy.

The Council's executive powers impair the Commission's ability to ensure the execution of the EU's laws, which it has shown itself well able to do in a field such as competition policy, where it has been given full responsibility. It has many attributes of a federal executive, but will not be fully effective unless it is given such powers across the board, subject to accountability to the legislature.

The federal elements in the EU institutions have enabled them to function to the benefit of the states and citizens. But if their interests are to be adequately served by a Union that will be enlarged to include 30 states or more, these federal elements will have to be strengthened.

The EC and its federal competences

If 'closer integration' means more effective and democratic institutions, we need it. But if it refers to further powers in the Union's main fields of activity, which are the economy and the environment, not much more is required.

The single market provides the framework for a modern market economy, and the external trade policy has made the Union an equal partner of the US in the world trade system. The single currency, though weakened by Britain's opt-out, goes far to complete the single market and gives the Union the potential to balance the US in the world financial system. The modest budget finances the Union as it stands at present, though more may be needed to respond to enlargement and growing external responsibilities. Over 200 laws deal with the cross-border problems of environmental pollution and the Union plays a leading part in international negotiations on global warming. So it has the potential to deal with the common interests of its states and citizens in these fields.

The other main field in which the member states lack the capacity for effective separate action is defence, where big responsibilities would be a competence too far for the Union, at least for now. NATO functions because of American hegemonic leadership, but there is no such hegemony among the European states. They can operate on a modest scale with instruments such as the Rapid Reaction Force. But they could give the Union major responsibility for defence only when it has developed solid and tested democratic institutions. Until such time, it can become a federal polity, but not a federal state.

Where the states can manage their own affairs effectively, the EU has no business to intervene. Central to this area is the welfare state, where the Union has generally not sought to interfere, though it has been given some minor powers in education, public health, and cultural affairs that should be returned to the states.

Thus a federal EU would not require much by way of additional competences, save in the field of external security, where its responsibilities could be developed by stages over a substantial period.

The alternative is dependence, not independence

The alternative to a federal Europe, capable of acting on behalf of its states and citizens, is dependence on America, in so far as we are lucky, and on impersonal or less benign external forces, in so far as we are not—though we British have the option of dependence on a federal Europe if our neighbours succeed in federating without us.

Domination by a single superpower, even by a democracy such as the US, creates a highly unstable world, good neither for the Americans nor for the rest of us; and it will be followed by a yet more unstable bipolarity between the US and China, unless a partnership between the US and a federal Europe is developed first, strong enough to underpin global institutions as the basis for a stable world order.

Tony Blair's call for the EU to become 'a superpower but not a superstate' is less fanciful than it may sound. The EU, with its quasi-federal arrangements for external trade, is already as great a trading power as the US. The euro gives it the potential for a similar role in the international monetary system, as it also has in the field of the environment. In defence the US will long remain supreme, though the EU can perform an increasingly important complementary role. But the Union can be an effective superpower in most other respects, provided that the federal elements in its institutions are strengthened.

The inter-governmentalist approach, treating the European Parliament and the Court of Justice as spare wheels and the Commission as a secretariat for an all-powerful Council of Ministers, cannot deliver an EU with the necessary stability and strength. Its advocates may believe themselves to be realists. But how can it be realistic to suppose that a hydra-headed collection of representatives of governments of up to 30 or more states can properly manage the Union's affairs? The democratic political systems of all those states will be centrifugal forces, pulling the Union apart at difficult moments in national or Union affairs, unless the Union itself is also endowed with a democratic system that can attract the citizens' support, alongside the commitment to their state.

It is illusory to suppose that all those representatives of democratically elected states' governments can themselves provide a transparent, democratic, and effective political system by horse-trading in Brussels. That, not the Union's federal elements, is the 'Brussels' which is insufficiently accountable and effective to serve the interests of European citizens in the way they should be served. The Union, with the federal elements it has already been given, has done far more for them than a purely intergovernmental system could have done. But it remains liable to stagnate or disintegrate unless it is made properly democratic and effective.

The key reforms are to give the European Parliament the right to co-decide all the laws and the budget, instead of just half of them; to give the Commission adequate executive power, with full accountability to the Parliament and Council; and to make the Council a more normal house of the states, holding its legislative sessions in public, generally voting by weighted majority, matters that are not now within the Commission's fields of competence. These reforms would go far to apply to the Union the principles of representative government.

Britain and a federal Union

British discussion of federalism has, in the past half-century, been lamentably superficial and inaccurate. Federalism has been regarded as a foreign idea. But the American founding fathers who invented the principle of democratic government at two levels were steeped in the British political tradition; the Westminster parliament enacted the federal constitutions of Australia, Canada, India, and Malaysia; and in the 1930s people such as William Beveridge, Lord Lothian, Lionel Robbins, and Barbara Wootton led an influential federalist movement. The federal idea is a product of British democratic and empirical political philosophy.

Federalism has been equated with a 'centralized superstate', distracting attention both from the need for joint government in fields that European governments can no longer manage separately and from the federal principle which provides for decentralization in all other fields.

It has even been asserted that 'federalism is dead'. But the European Central Bank and the euro are among the most important federal elements established in the Union so far; the German foreign minister Joschka Fischer speaks for a federalist political class when he envisages a federal 'centre of gravity' in the Union; and his view is widely supported in other member states.

Not only is federalism alive, but a federal Union is as necessary for the British as for other Europeans. The economic, environmental, and security needs apply to us as they do to the others. The arguments for democratic federal institutions are at least as strong. For if the principles of liberal democracy, which the British did so much to develop, are not applied in the fields where states such as ours can no longer function effectively, democracy will be weakened as citizens come to realize that it cannot satisfy their needs. If the British government promotes the key federal reforms, it will, given the support available in other member states, have a very good chance of success. Political discourse should rise above the level of slogans and give due weight to the benefits a federal Union could bring to our people.

A LARGER, STRONGER, MORE DEMOCRATIC EUROPE

Tony Blair

The following is extracted from the speech Tony Blair made in Warsaw on 6 October 2000, setting out his views on the development of the European Union.

The most important challenge for Europe is to wake up to the new reality: Europe is widening and deepening simultaneously. There will be more of us in the future, trying to do more.

The issue is: not whether we do this, but how we reform this new Europe so that it both delivers real benefits to the people of Europe, addressing the priorities they want addressed, and does so in a way that has their consent and support.

There are two opposite models so far proposed. One is Europe as a free trade area, like NAFTA in North America. This is the model beloved by British Conservatives. The other is the classic federalist model, in which Europe elects its Commission president and the

European Parliament becomes the true legislative European body and Europe's principal democratic check.

The difficulty with the first is that it nowhere near answers what our citizens expect from Europe, besides being wholly unrealistic politically. In a Europe with a single market and single currency, there will inevitably be a need for closer economic coordination. In negotiations over world trade and global finance, Europe is stronger if it speaks with one voice.

In areas like the environment and organized crime, in policing our borders, Europe needs to work together. In foreign and security policy, though nations will guard jealously their own national interests, there are times when it will be of clear benefit to all that Europe acts and speaks together. What people want from Europe is more than just free trade. They want prosperity, security, and strength.

In a world with the power of the USA, with new alliances to be made with the neighbours of Europe like Russia, developing nations with vast populations like India and China, Japan, not just an economic power but a country that will rightly increase its political might too—with the world increasingly forming powerful regional blocs (ASEAN, Mercosur)—Europe's citizens need Europe to be strong and united. They need it to be a power in the world. Whatever its origin, Europe today is no longer just about peace. It is about projecting collective power. That is one very clear reason, quite apart from the economic reasons, why the Central European nations want to join.

So a limited vision of Europe does not remotely answer the modern demands people place on Europe.

The difficulty, however, with the view of Europe as a superstate, subsuming nations into a politics dominated by supranational institutions, is that it too fails the test of the people. There are issues of democratic accountability in Europe—the so-called democratic deficit. But we can spend hours on end trying to devise a perfect form of European democracy and get nowhere. The truth is the primary sources of democratic accountability in Europe are the directly elected and representative institutions of the nations of Europe—national parliaments and governments. That is not to say Europe will not in future generations develop its own strong demos or polity, but it hasn't yet.

And let no one be in any doubt: nations like Poland, who struggled so hard to achieve statehood, whose citizens shed their blood in that cause, are not going to give it up lightly. We should celebrate our diverse cultures and identities, our distinctive attributes as nations.

Europe is a Europe of free, independent sovereign nations, who choose to pool that sovereignty in pursuit of their own interests and the common good, achieving more together than we can achieve alone. The EU will remain a unique combination of the inter-governmental and the supranational. Such a Europe can, in its economic and political strength, be a superpower; a superpower, but not a superstate.

We should not therefore begin with an abstract discussion of institutional change. We begin with the practical question: What should Europe do? What do the people of Europe want and expect it to do? Then we focus Europe and its institutions around the answer.

- How we complete the single market.
- How we drive through necessary economic reform.
- How we phase out the wasteful and inefficient aspects of the CAP.
- How we restore full employment.
- How we get a more coherent foreign policy.
- How we develop the military capability we require without which common defence policy is a chimera.
- How we fight organized crime, immigration racketeering, the drugs trade.
- How we protect an environment that knows no borders.
- And of course, how we stop Europe focusing on things that it doesn't need to do, the interfering part of Europe that antagonizes even Europe's most ardent supporters.

The problem Europe's citizens have with Europe arises when Europe's priorities aren't theirs. No amount of institutional change—most of which passes them by completely—will change that. Reforming Europe to give it direction and momentum around the people's priorities will. The citizens of Europe must feel that they own Europe, not that Europe owns them. So let me turn to the changes I believe are part of delivering that direction.

First, we owe it to our citizens to let them know clearly what policies and laws are being enacted in their name.

The European Council, bringing together all the heads of government, is the final court of appeal from other councils of ministers unable to reconcile national differences.

That is a vital role. But the European Council should above all be the body which sets the agenda of the Union. Indeed, formally in the Treaty of Rome, that is the task given to it. We now have European Council meetings every three months. And in truth they do—for example, in areas like the Luxembourg summit on jobs, the Lisbon summit on economic reform, the Poertschach summit on defence—develop the future political direction of Europe. I would like to propose that we do this in a far more organized and structured way.

Just as governments go before their electorates and set out their agenda for the coming years, so must the European Council do the same. We need to do it in all the crucial fields of European action: economic, foreign policy, defence, and the fight against cross-border crime. I am proposing today an annual agenda for Europe, set by the European Council.

The president of the Commission is a member of the European Council, and would play his full part in drawing up the agenda. He would then bring a proposal for heads of government to debate, modify, and endorse. It would be a clear legislative, as well as political, programme setting the workload of individual councils. The Commission's independence as guardians of the treaty would be unchanged. And the Commission would still bring forward additional proposals where its role as guardian of those treaties so required. But we would have clear political direction, a programme and a timetable by which all the institutions would be guided.

We should be open too to reforming the way individual councils work, perhaps through team presidencies that give the leadership of the Council greater continuity and weight; greater use of elected chairs of councils and their working groups; and ensuring that the secretary-general of the Council, Javier Solana, can play his full role in the development of foreign and defence policy. For example, when Europe is more than 25 members, can we seriously believe that a country will hold the presidency only every 12 or 13 years? But two or three countries together, with a mix of large and small states, might make greater sense. In future we may also need a better way of overseeing and monitoring the Union's programme than the three-monthly European Councils.

Second, there is an important debate about a constitution for Europe. In practice I suspect that, given the sheer diversity and complexity of the EU, its constitution, like the British constitution, will continue to be found in a number of different treaties, laws, and precedents. It is perhaps easier for the British than for others to recognize that a constitutional debate must not necessarily end with a single, legally binding document called a constitution for an entity as dynamic as the EU.

What I think is both desirable and realistic is to draw up a statement of the principles according to which we should decide what is best done at the European level and what should be done at the national level, a kind of charter of competences. This would allow countries too to define clearly what is then done at a regional level. This Statement of Principles would be a political, not a legal, document. It could therefore be much simpler and more accessible to Europe's citizens.

I also believe that the time has now come to involve representatives of national parliaments more on such matters, by creating a second chamber of the European Parliament.

A second chamber's most important function would be to review the EU's work, in the light of this agreed Statement of Principles. It would not get involved in the day-to-day negotiation of legislation — that is properly the role of the existing European Parliament. Rather, its task would be to help implement the agreed Statement of Principles; so that we do what we need to do at a European level but also so that we devolve power downwards. Whereas a formal constitution would logically require judicial review by a European constitutional court, this would be political review by a body of democratically elected politicians. It would be dynamic rather than static, allowing for change in the application of these principles without elaborate legal revisions every time.

Such a second chamber could also, I believe, help provide democratic oversight at a European level of the common foreign and security policy.

Efficient decision making in an enlarged Union will also mean more enhanced cooperation. I have no problem with greater flexibility or groups of member states going forward together. But that must not lead to a hard core; a Europe in which some member states create their own set of shared policies and institutions from which others are in practice excluded. Such groups must at every stage be open to others who wish to join.

RULED BY FOREIGNERS

Boris Johnson

The liberation of Kosovo. What a business. No one who was in Pristina that June day, as the Irish Guards rolled in, will forget the jubilation on the faces of the Albanians. Out of the cellars they came, out of the forests where they had been hiding while NATO bombed the place from 30,000 feet, and they stood by the sides of the roads, weeping and cheering. They climbed aboard the tanks and they kissed the squaddies, and they went into the gardens of the Serbs and plundered the roses and threw innumerable red petals around. And why were they so exultant? Not just because they had ended the oppression of the dreaded purple-pyjamaed Mupmen; not just because it was an end to the pogroms and the beatings.

The Kosovar Albanians were that day celebrating something for which the Kosovo Liberation Army has been fighting for years, the end of their bogus 'autonomous' status within the Federal Republic of Yugoslavia and the first steps towards self-rule. Now their students would take examinations in their own language, and be governed by their own kind. As I consulted them on their emotions, it struck me how important it is, in a functioning democracy, to feel some sort of allegiance to the people who rule you. It seems to be a fact of human nature. That tie may be expressed in a shared language, or just a shared sense of nationhood. But it seems to be essential for a successful polity. Countless wars of liberation show what happens when the bond, the mutual loyalty between rulers and ruled, does not exist.

The Kosovar Albanians ended up with no sense of community with Belgrade; and that, pretty much, is the problem with the EU as it is presently constituted, and that is why, in due time, I believe it may sustain some sort of rupture — not as violent as the Yugoslav wars, no, nothing like, but an embarrassing popular reaction to the loss of democratic legitimacy. The problem with the EU, bluntly, is that we are ruled by foreigners; charming, principled, well-meaning foreigners, but foreigners nonetheless. This means that try as we may, we find it hard to rid ourselves of the suspicion that their primary loyalty is not to us, but to their own country, and that they may sometimes take decisions — and in a language we may not understand — which on balance may suit them more than they suit us.

When I say we are ruled by them, I mean exactly that. We elect politicians under our system, and we send them to the House of Commons, and then we find they are overruled by 'Brussels', where Brussels means the ministers of the rest of the EU countries, meeting in secret, and sometimes actually outvoting our government representative. There is no need to rehearse here the tropes of euroscepticism, the harmonization programmes which cause such delicious outrage. I will say nothing about the plan that British chocolate should be rechristened vegelate, the attempt to ban the prawn cocktail flavour crisp, the plunder of our fish. Suffice it to say that there is always a grain of truth — usually more than a grain — in what the Foreign Office calls the 'Euro-myths'. You do not have to be Christopher Booker to believe that everywhere, up the creeks and inlets, flows the tide of European law.

Take a scheme called English Partnerships, invented by the Major government, by which developers were encouraged to invest in run-down inner-city areas. Since it would cost more to improve the site than the site would ultimately be worth, the government undertook to make up the difference, and also added a small element of profit for the developer. This innocent scheme was first approved by the EU Commission, but then thrown out in 1999 by Mario Monti, the commissioner responsible for competition, on the ground that it was illegal state aid. The House of Commons Select Committee for Environment, Transport and the Regions became enraged. What business was it of Brussels, they demanded. This was a wholly domestic scheme, they fumed, with no trading implications. But what could they do? They were only the democratically elected politicians of Britain.

These injustices are nothing compared to the erosion of sovereignty envisaged in EMU. Look at the poor Irish, who are told by the envious powers around the table in the Ecofin (the meeting of economic and finance ministers) that they must raise their business taxes, and sharpish. The

Irish, you will recall, are experiencing inflationary difficulties caused by the sacrifice of their monetary independence. As the eunuched governor of the Irish central bank complained, he can no longer set interest rates to suit Irish circumstances. Therefore, says Brussels, the Irish must lose not just their monetary independence, but their fiscal independence as well. Imagine if Britain found herself—as she well might—in the same circumstances.

What is the point of Westminster, a parliament that came of age in a row about the right to determine the levels of taxation, if that power no longer resides there? It was a slogan of the American War of Independence that there should be no taxation without representation.

There is a real risk, at some future moment in our membership of the deepening Union, that the British people, having been dared and shoved and pushed around, will revolt, or at least express their grievances in some moderately truculent fashion. The problem, to repeat, is that they don't feel the slightest allegiance to the EU's federal institutions. There is no tie of respect or custom. If you asked them whether the European Parliament was in Strasbourg or Brussels or Luxembourg, they wouldn't have a clue (the answer is all three, by the way, dummkopf).

If the Kosovar Albanians had felt strongly loyal to Belgrade, and to the federal institutions, then all might have been well. Similarly, if we all had a strong sense of loyalty to the institutions of Europe, the problem of democratic illegitimacy would scarcely arise. If we all felt truly

European, then the problem posed by EMU would be less acute. The people of Tyne and Wear endure the interest rates set by the Bank of England, which are largely designed to control inflation in the south-east; and they endure them because they accept that Britain is a single polity, and that it may be necessary that they should endure more acute conditions in their area, for the good of the whole.

The problem with EMU is that it requires us all to imagine we are a province of this country called Europe; and if the macroeconomic decisions (interest rates, tax) taken are not in the interests of our country, well, then that is too bad, because it is all in the wider interests of our Euro-patrie.

That would be fine if people had a genuine European consciousness. But they don't, to a surprising degree. I often ask school audiences whether they feel British or European, or British first and European second, and they always say British first, and everything else pretty much nowhere. You see a couple of fluttering hands coyly suggesting that they feel additionally or secondarily European. But I've never talked to an audience at school or university where anyone felt primarily European. Perhaps in a hundred years time our descendants will say that they are, in the phrase of Jean Monnet, in mind European, but I see no sign of it yet.

That is why the absence of democracy in the European institutions, the setting of national parliaments at naught, is so vicious and so corrupting. The answer of the federalists is to admit that things are not going on quite as fast as they would like, but that if they build the institutions like EMU, then perhaps this vital European political consciousness will grow. The general plan seems to be to keep festooning the place with Euro-flags, and to keep adorning our number plates and our roadsigns, and perhaps—they hope—public sentiment will catch up.

To which I say, it is taking some time, and in the meantime you are making a mockery of democracy, and in any case, WHY? What is the purpose of this whole exercise, 50 years after the Second World War, 10 years after the end of the Cold War? Why do you want to build this tightly drawn EU superstate, this white man's laager on the western appendix of the Eurasian landmass? You get some odd mumbled answers. Some say it is all to do with 'standing up to' America or China or Japan, though it is not quite clear why it is in our interests to 'stand up' to these places, rather than trade peaceably with them. Others, more honestly, say that federalism is an end in itself, a genuine and visionary desire to rebuild the western half of the Roman empire. Well, I say phooey. Who is the emperor in this setup? Romano Prodi? It is deeply undemocratic. You are asking people to be ruled by institutions and people to whom they have no sense of kinship or allegiance. You are risking a hell of a backlash; of course it will be nothing like as bad as Yugoslavia, but then why on earth take the risk?

SIX HERETICAL PROPOSALS

Mark Leonard

For those on the outside looking in, democracy is the EU's greatest prize. Former dissidents such as Vaclav Havel have spent their entire lives coaxing their compatriots to meet the standards exacted by the EU. But within the EU's borders, the Union is presented as the most serious threat to national democracy, and many have pointed out that it would not be allowed to join itself because it does not meet the democratic criteria it sets for its own members. Welcome to the paradox of democracy!

The EU's next 'grand projet' will have to be democracy. The Danish 'nej' in their referendum on the euro showed that political arguments are as important as economic ones. They will be the key to bringing our citizens with us as we try to make a success of enlargement and the single currency. The German foreign minister Joschka Fischer's recent speeches show that democracy is racing up the political agenda, but unfortunately the debate is being conducted in precisely the wrong way.

First, his call for the EU to become a federation of states plays into sceptic hands by making EU democracy a threat to national democracy. Second, Fischer demands the same standard of legitimacy for EU institutions as for national governments. Yet the EU is very different from an embryonic nation-state. Its power comes from its form as a network of national governments that sometimes cooperate to meet shared objectives and at other times compete. It will never ask people to pay direct taxes (its budget is less than 1.5 per cent of the Union's GDP compared to national governments which all spend over 40 per cent); and citizens will not have to risk their lives for it (soldiers in the Rapid Reaction Force will be members of national forces not a European Army). So it makes no sense to try to legitimate it in the same way as national governments.

But the biggest problem with federal models of democracy is not just that the EU is different from a nation-state in construction: it is that democracy is itself changing. It is ironic that at a time when national democratic systems are under pressure all over the world, people like Joschka Fischer are calling on us to go back to eighteenth-century models of democracy and force the EU into a straitjacket built for another age. Turnout in elections is falling across the EU, cynicism with mainstream politics is on the rise, and all representative forms of government are struggling to connect. It is time to turn the debate about democracy in Europe on its head and look not just at how national parliaments can help legitimate the EU, but also at how Europe can help plug the national democratic deficit.

This is an area where the UK can take the lead. Paradoxically our experience of euroscepticism and the lively debate we have had about legitimacy—coupled with our long history of democracy and recent democratic reforms—mean that we can offer a lot to this debate. I will make six heretical proposals which try to shift the debate out of the federalist tramlines it has got stuck in.

First, member states should create a commissioner for democracy. We should copy the example of Sweden, which has a minister for democracy, and charge a commissioner with pioneering different ways of communicating with citizens. This person could be charged with gathering best practice from around the world, exploring how IT can be used to develop forms of governance that are more responsive to citizens, re-examining the roles of the Committee of the Regions and the Economic and Social Committee, finding ways of improving accountability on European issues at a national level, and promoting good democratic practice across member states and EU institutions. The democracy commissioner should lead a quest to find the most effective and innovative ways of linking public policy back to the public. This would mark a powerful symbolic commitment from the top and show real determination to change the EU's relationship with its citizens.

Second, we must understand that most citizens worry more about outcomes than processes. Political systems exist to match public policy to citizens' priorities by making trade-offs between competing interests and bundling them into strategic programmes which voters can choose between. Within Europe many of the things that we want depend on common action. But the gulf between what people expect from the EU (solutions to cross-border problems) and what they get (the Common Agricultural Policy) is much more damaging than the formal democratic deficit. We need a change of culture that puts delivery at the top of everyone's agenda. We must flesh out the idea of government by objectives as well as directives which started with the employment targets set in Luxembourg. The EU must set itself timed objectives in all the areas that matter most to its citizens and then work out clear ways to drive progress (see point four below).

Third, we must transform the debate about subsidiarity. To restore legitimacy in the institutions we need to find ways of proving that the EU will only act in areas where it can add value. This must be shown symbolically by changing the preamble to the treaty so that it no longer commits us to 'ever closer union'. And in practical terms one of the driving principles of subsidiarity should be that each level must earn the right to govern by proving that it can do it better than the centre. There are many things that the EU should be better placed to do than the nation-state, such as the delivery of overseas aid, but it is failing. We need to move beyond the federal model of allocating exclusive responsibility for different tasks to different tiers of government by function and explore how we can set shared objectives centrally and see the different tiers of government working together to achieve them.

Fourth, we must find ways of mobilizing the power of the 'European average'. Once there are clearly set objectives, we will need accountability and transparency to ensure that they are met and that the different tiers of government pull together behind these goals. It is a provocative thought, but it is possible a European statistics office could do more for political accountability in Europe than a directly elected European Parliament. Access to comparative European figures on prices, taxes, economic performance, and public services has vastly increased accountability for national governments. The reason the recent fuel crisis sparked such animosity was not just the level of prices consumers faced in the UK but the fact that British consumers could see that they were paying above the European average. The fact that people see their national policies within a broader context is creating a genuine competition for policies across Europe.

The fifth signpost has to be reinventing representation to deliver competition between policies. Instead of seeing EU politics as a bolt-on extra that can be confined to the European Parliament, we need to ensure that the political debate runs through all the EU institutions and member states. The biggest challenge is reforming the European Council so that it can give political direction to the whole EU system — and create the clear objectives that we need if we are going to succeed.

The Council is the EU institution with the most power and legitimacy because it contains Europe's best-known and most powerful political leaders. They lead political parties as well as national governments, and they must start treating the European Council as a political forum for strategic debate as well as somewhere to defend their national interests. By acting as a more political body, the European Council can develop tools for strategic decision-making and leadership, and provide the political and policy framework for the Commission's legislative, financial, and administrative proposals.

We will need some institutional changes to make this happen, such as replacing the six-monthly rotating presidency with one that can deliver leadership for a longer period of time. One idea might be for governments to elect a three-country team presidency (one for each pillar) for a two-year period. We will also need to create a back-up for the Council in the form of a new Council of Europe, consisting of ministers with deputy prime minister status who would meet monthly in Brussels and coordinate the work of the different councils of ministers to ensure that a co-strategic agenda is being followed through. But the biggest change will be cultural: focusing on the big picture and providing leadership rather than getting sucked into the minutiae of day-to-day horse-trading.

Finally, we must explore direct democracy. Improving representative democracy will make an enormous difference to the effectiveness and legitimacy of the EU. It will make the EU system more strategic and allow citizens to see a link between the way they vote in national elections and the policies being pursued at a European level. But it will not be enough in the long term: people will also want a more direct way of participating and voting for what we want Europe to do.

Because the EU will never have a single government or president that citizens can vote out, we should consider supplementing representative politics with forums of direct democracy. In the long term, we could explore the idea of holding Europe-wide referendums giving citizens the chance to overturn an existing piece of EU legislation or to put a new legislative issue on the agenda in policy areas of EU competence. We should also investigate the idea of a 'European People's Panel', which policy-makers in both the EU's institutions or in national governments can draw upon to test public attitudes to what the EU's priorities should be, and how service delivery can be improved from the point of view of the user.

These are just a few ways of reframing the democracy debate. They all try to develop thinking that is appropriate for a network of nation-states in an age of globalization and the internet, rather than trying to force Europe into the structures of eighteenth-century states.

10 CULTURE AND IDENTITY

Most of this book is about matters of policy: politics, economics, diplomacy, and social and environmental conditions. But our attitudes to these matters may be heavily influenced by deeper questions of our feelings of identity. This depends on our culture in the widest sense (from film and literature to sport and food), our personal connections, our own experiences—and to what extent we feel that we are part of Europe or alternatively that Europe is foreign to us.

BRITAIN'S CULTURAL PLACE IN EUROPE

Philip Dodd

It's a fix: the title of this collection rigs the answer. In the phrase 'Britain and Europe', the 'and' is the equivalent of an English Channel that we are invited to cross, or not, depending on our political loyalties and understanding. Britain can choose to be in Europe, the title says.

But, in cultural terms, that seems mere historical illiteracy: Britain and Europe have been and are Siamese twins. John Constable, that quintessentially English painter (and no, I'm not confusing British and English) is unimaginable outside his dialogue with the French landscape painter Claude—just as much as Arsenal is now inconceivable without French stars such as Patrick Vieira, or British daily life without Italian food, our favourite cuisine. Even a glory of British 1970s television such as *Play for Today* acknowledged its debt to the revolutionary grammar of the French Nouvelle Vague, with its handheld cameras and commitment to contemporary urban life. Signs of Britain's promiscuity can be seen all around us in the streets, whether in the city of Edinburgh, where Tony

Blair's old school, Fettes College, is designed as a French chateau, or in Blackpool, where the Tower is a clone of the Eiffel Tower.

But the flow of influence between Europe and Britain has always been two-way. Voltaire, one of the intellectual architects of the French Revolution, worshipped at the feet of English liberty; British fashion designers are just as much at the heart of European fashion now as they were in the 1930s, when a British woman ruled Paris fashion; Shakespeare has haunted German drama from Goethe to Brecht; the Welsh footballer John Charles was an Italian national hero in the 1960s, when he played for Juventus; and the Scottish Enlightenment was a major event in European intellectual life, helping to remodel later European thought. At a more anecdotal level, this morning I have received a generous e-mail from the German director of a major arts complex who speaks of 'referring to Britain as an example'.

What's at stake is not Britain's cultural place in Europe — that's self-evident, at least that's my position — but why it continues to be necessary to have to make an argument about Britain-in-Europe and Europe-in-Britain.

Now I know that by Europe this collection actually means the EU and I'm apparently talking about another Europe, an 'imagined community', to use Benedict Anderson's phrase. But until we understand Britain-in-Europe, we can't even begin to have a serious discussion about Britain and the EU.

At present, discussions of Europe in Britain are rarely more, and often less, than debates about economics (the euro) and politics (Brussels bureaucracy). While these issues are clearly critical—it does matter whether the EU can deliver material prosperity and whether its institutions are democratically accountable—the political and economic frame of reference isn't, by itself, sufficient. If European is to be an identity inhabited by the British, then this identity must be able to provide them with stories which help them to make sense of more than the political part of their lives.

Unfortunately it's the stories available about Britain's relationship with Europe that are the problem. Of recent prime ministers, Margaret Thatcher best understood the power of stories—that they can compel and, at times, enthral people; have a past and future as well as a present tense; have heroes and enemies; and can orchestrate elements of the national life and history, often contradictory ones, and give them a persuasive coherence.

Margaret Thatcher's Britishness was singular, not plural; it was enough to be 'one of them' by not being 'one of us'. Her Britishness was predicated on a sustained process of purification and exclusion. During her regime, according to her narrative, a proud and self-sufficient Britain was surrounded by enemies, internal and external, as it had been in the past—and 'Europe' was cast as one of those enemies and, after the defeat of Galtieri in the Falklands War, the most dangerous one.

Philip Dodd

Of course Margaret Thatcher was hardly the first to identify Britain's proud self-sufficiency, or to define Britishness
in terms of its difference from continental Europe. The
historian Linda Colley has been persuasive in demonstrat-
ing how important Protestantism was in the eighteenth
century in helping to unify the various groups within
Britain by marking out their difference from continental
Europe.

The problem for the present Labour administration is that,
although it has apparently rejected Thatcher's story of
national purity versus European contamination (one that
continues to be rehashed by William Hague and the
eurosceptics), it is failing to provide an alternative, compelling story of Britain-in-Europe which can help the government and the people make sense of the government's
policy initiatives and choices within the EU.

If a cultural address to the relationship between Britain
and Europe makes nonsense of the vision of Fortress
Britain fending off unwanted advances from the foreigners
across the seas, such an address also has the virtue of
demolishing the idea of a Fortress Europe. After all, the
briefest glance at European history would show that, from
the time of Columbus, Europe's sense of itself has been
shaped by engagement with — and sometimes subjugation
of — large parts of the rest of the world. It is simply impossible, or ought to be, to think of the history and identity of
France outside of its relationship with North Africa, Spain
outside of its relationship with Latin America, or Britain
outside of its relationship with India. And what about other

countries, such as Turkey or Russia, which have as often belonged to the history of Asia as of Europe?

The tragedy is that no one would recognize this ever-changing, promiscuous Europe in the cloud of arguments that has enveloped Brussels and the EU. The rest of the world can apparently go hang, while one side of the argument claims that Europe (the Union) has become a synonym for an over-centralized and wasteful superstate, denying national sovereignty to its members, while the other argues that Brussels can deliver answers to economic and social questions that can no longer be tackled by the nation-state.

What the briefest excursion into the cultural history and present of Europe illuminates, and this has been the briefest of journeys, is a radically different story of Europe. If my argument is accepted, then it's impossible to pretend that Britain isn't already in Europe, or that it was ever not. But the Britain and the Europe that I see as twins are unrecognizable to both the purist British eurosceptics and the centralizing Brussels administrators.

In the story I am proposing, both Britain and Europe are outward-looking, ready to change and to learn and unlearn; there is intercourse across Europe, a mixing and mingling, in which the British have played their full part. But there is no uniformity or homogeneity. Constable belongs no less to the culture of his particular time and place because he is umbilically attached to other places. Patrick Vieira plays for the French national team and for the English team Arsenal. In this story, the settled geography of the Cold War Europe, divided into East and West, is seen as an aberration, less representative of the 'mixing and mingling Europe' than Joseph Conrad and Apollinaire, Bartok and Janaček, those 'eastern' Europeans who are among the originators of 'western' European modernism.

Such a story of Britain-in-Europe would both make the sceptics look the lobotomized folk they are, yet give the government criteria against which to judge the trajectory of the EU. Such a story would make enlargement common sense — after all, East and West had dialogue with one another long before the Cold War. It would also dismantle the myth that movement across Europe or between Europe and other parts of the world is something novel and would at least allow Europeans to have an honest debate about immigration into Europe, rather than live by the myth that until recently there was a settled number of inviolable nation-states that made up Europe. It would illuminate how much hybrids have to offer Europe in the future, as they have in the past. It would make clear that the centralizing habits of Brussels mask another more creative version of Europe — one not afraid of integration, but one where integration licenses diversity rather than homogeneity.

But, above all, what this story would do would be to provide European citizens, whether in Britain or elsewhere, with an account of Europe that speaks to a larger history than that provided by either pro- or anti-EU lobbies — a story which belongs to all of those of us who have lived and live in Europe, and not merely to our political masters.

THE DIPLOMACY OF THE HEART

Michael Elliott

There are eight houses on my street in suburban New York. Across the road from me lives an American investment banker, who has just returned from a four-year tour in the City. Next door to him lives a Scot, the CEO of his own American firm. Then there's the American advertising executive, who graduated from the American School in London, and whose agency is now owned by a British firm. And there's my wife and myself, who have spent more than half our working life in the US and whose children, seemingly effortlessly, regard themselves as both British and American.

We are all, if you like, 'Nylons', the term that *Newsweek* magazine coined in 2000 for the growing number of professionals whose life straddles the cities of London and New York. But we are also, perhaps, exemplars of a more significant phenomenon—the old and continuing interpenetration of British and American life. As Britain faces elemental choices in its relationship with the nations of Europe, it is appropriate to examine the depth of the

Atlantic link, and to wonder if it hurts — or helps — resolve questions of British policy.

Let me be clear at the outset on the focus of this. I am not concerned here with the 'special relationship,' at least as it is commonly understood as a set of agreed assumptions in foreign and security policy. Reasonable people may differ as to the importance of that relationship (though few can doubt that it is a term used far more in London than Washington.) Nor do I want to argue that, as a political matter, there is or should be some sacred bond between Britain and the US that is more valuable than any links that may be forged with Europe. My subject is the diplomacy of the heart; the network of personal, economic, and social links that bind two nations together and that act more at the level of individual preferences than at that of political decision-making.

The Anglo-American link is of course nearly 400 years old, and it was not sundered by the War of Independence. Indeed, the founding fathers of the American republic explicitly based their claims on British precedents and founded their ideologies on British models. From Bolingbroke, Wilkes, and the eighteenth-century British opposition to the Hanoverian state to Hume, Adam Smith, and the Scottish establishment, the founding fathers took succour and ideas from British sources.

Throughout the history of the republic, certain shared habits have naturally made it easy for Americans and Britons to understand each other. Foremost among those factors, naturally, is language, but they also include legal systems based on the common law, and—perhaps—a belief in the revealed truth of classical economics, with its insistence on the wonders of the invisible hand of the market, free trade, constitutional constraints on taxation, and a suspicion of Colbertist dirigisme.

More recently, it is often argued that the experience of the Second World War, when Britain and the US made up the democratic two-thirds of the alliance against Fascism, and when hundreds of thousands of American troops were billeted in Britain, cemented an emotional bond between the two peoples. (That case, though, needs some qualification. America and Americans were not universally popular in wartime Britain; for every GI bride there was an ill-paid British squaddie who found the Americans overbearing and rude. For their part, American policy-makers did not take away from the war such warm and fuzzy feelings for their cousins as to incline them to contemplate a post-war Anglo-American condominium. Dean Acheson and the other wise men of the Truman administration were convinced that the British decision to stand apart, in high condescension, from the European Coal and Steel Community was an error of tragic proportions.)

In our own times, ease of transport and communications, coupled with the particular development of the British economy, have deepened the links. To all intents and purposes, there is an hourly air shuttle between London and New York. Britons have developed a comparative expertise in those sectors of the service economy in which the use of language counts for most—advertising, finance, media and publishing, and to some extent information technology. If Britain had been any good at textile manufacturing or mechanical engineering, its best and brightest would have found careers in Turin or Munich. It isn't, so they head for New York and Los Angeles instead, helping to build a single, English-speaking, North Atlantic service economy. Martin Amis is more of a typical Brit than, one suspects, he thinks he is.

The extent of British emigration to the US, indeed, is the hidden flywheel that drives the diplomacy of the heart. Among European peoples, the British history of emigration is unique. There has never been one period of mass British emigration to the US — so nothing to approximate the German experience after 1848, the Irish one after the famine, or the wave of Italian emigration between 1890 and 1910. Nor is there any distinctive 'British–American' cultural memory in the way that there is, say, an 'Italian–American' one; the common language made assimilation into the US much easier for Britons than for anyone else. On the other hand, the British have never stopped emigrating to America; unlike other Europeans, they have just kept coming, in a steady stream, for 300 years. In 1960, for example, there were more than 1.2 million residents of the US who had been born in Italy compared with 833,000 born in the UK. By 1990, however, there were just 580,000 Italian-born Americans, compared with 640,000 born in the UK. In recent years, Britain has routinely provided twice as many legal immigrants to the US as any other west European country.

The strangely ignored history of British emigration is not, of course, solely about the US; it encompasses other places where the flag of empire once flew. But because the British overwhelmingly have left and continue to leave for English-speaking countries, emigration works to limit the personal contacts that ordinary Britons have with the countries of continental Europe. A quotidian expression of the diplomacy of the heart is to ask the question 'Where do you telephone on Christmas Day?' For the British, the answer has traditionally been: 'Not Europe.' There are now countless British families with an Uncle Harry or Aunty Flo in San Diego or Sydney; a son or daughter taking a gap year in Auckland or Oregon. (And increasingly, to add spice to the dish without destroying its flavour, a cousin Sudip studying in Bangalore.)

These various factors give rise to two questions. First, has the diplomacy of the heart made it more difficult to develop a coherent European policy? And second, are those factors likely to be as strong in the future as they have been in the past?

I think that the answer to the first is self-evident. Yes, the depth of personal links with the US (and other English-speaking nations) has indeed caused problems for the European policies of successive governments. The point here isn't the cost of New Zealand lamb and butter, which caused the Heath government such agony at the time of accession to the European Community. Nor do we need to dwell on the fact—true though it may be—that continental European countries drew very different lessons from the catastrophe of the Second World War than did never-occupied Britain. It is simply the case that for generations of Britons, the US has become, to an extent, familiar; Europe, by contrast, is 'foreign'. Aunty Flo and Uncle Harry don't live there; nor do Europe's television programmes and movies form part of the background noise of British culture. Only in the deepest recesses of London's media and political village can it be believed that such personal experiences don't matter.

Yet whether this state of affairs is an unchangeable feature of the British landscape is a much harder question to answer. In many ways, the US is a very foreign country — in its social habits, its brutal penal policies, its religiosity, its sports, its relative lack of social democratic safety-nets. Moreover, the US is not what it once was; for 25 years, it has seen mass emigration on a scale not witnessed for a century, which has made it a more Latino, more Asian society than formerly. At the same time, the web of shared experiences that link Britain to Europe are manifestly growing in strength. In summer 2000, it was claimed that half a million British families now own or rent property in France. The Channel Tunnel, European stars playing for British football teams, techno music and weekends in Ibiza — to say nothing of political opinions shared throughout Europe, like a commitment to global environmentalism — all work to bind Britons more closely to European attitudes and dreams than once seemed possible.

America will always be a lure; it is too glittering, too generous, too damn big for it to be otherwise. But whether it will continue to magnetize British public opinion as it has in the past, and work so as to diminish the chances of a wholehearted British commitment to the European project, must now be in some doubt.

11 THE VIEW FROM THE CONTINENT

When John Major returned from the negotiations at Maastricht in 1991 proudly brandishing the British opt-out on the 'Social Chapter', a Downing Street spokesman famously proclaimed it was 'game, set, and match' to Britain. The remark was attributed to Major and is still remembered in some European circles as typifying what they see as Britain's adversarial, them-and-us approach. For those who regret this, some despair that Britain will ever really commit itself to being at the heart of Europe, while others still hope.

Part of the problem for Britain has been that the real heart of Europe has traditionally been the powerful Franco-German axis which has driven the development of the EU. Recently this has been showing some signs of strain. One aspect of this was the debate sparked off by the important speech in May 2000 at Humboldt by the German foreign minister Joschka Fischer. He proclaimed ' "Quo vadis Europa?" is the question posed once again by the history of our continent', and answered his question with a personal integrationist vision of a European federation with a directly elected president of the Commission. This produced strong disagreement from the French.

The tensions in the Franco-German axis have helped to raise the issue of what alliances Britain may forge. Over the past couple of years there has been some talk of an alliance between Britain and Italy, the two other large countries. Although these two countries have often been diametrically opposed, they have found some common ground recently on issues like defence.

But while some forces on the continent want to bring Britain deeper into Europe, there are also eurosceptics who see Britain as a natural ally. The country which has raised the eurosceptic flag highest is what some have called 'plucky little Denmark'. In 1992 the Danish narrowly voted in a referendum to reject the Maastricht Treaty (although they accepted it a year later after they were given various opt-out rights). Then last year the Danes again voted narrowly not to take part in the single currency. Many eurosceptics are keen to stress they regard themselves as anti-EU or against some of the EU's manifestations and not as anti-European or anti-foreigner. They wish to build an international solidarity among eurosceptics, in which the British contingent would play a prominent part.

REAL DEMOCRACY, NOT A SOCIAL SCIENCE PROJECT

Jens-Peter Bonde

The cornerstone of any parliamentary democracy is the people's ability to elect representatives to parliament and then to have new laws passed or old ones repealed, always subject to their critical appraisal. A new parliament can always change the laws of the old parliament. This is what elections are all about.

If we only had the right to elect new politicians but not the right to amend or repeal bad laws, we could hardly claim to have democratic government, but this is precisely how the EU works with its process of qualified majority voting. Yes, we can still elect politicians to participate in EU law-making, but we can never amend laws when the competence to do so has been transferred from Westminster and the other national parliaments of Europe to the EU. We have already lost this essential component of our democracy. The Treaty of Nice will further erode our democratic say by adding 34 new articles to the qualified majority voting process and by introducing a new method called 'enhanced cooperation'.

Under the Nice Treaty the UK will give up one Commissioner and, in return, get 29 out of 237 votes in the Council of Ministers. From January 2005, 169 votes will be needed to pass a law with a qualified majority. If this qualified majority in the Council cannot be gathered, you cannot pass a new law or even amend an existing law. Call for a general election in the UK if you will, and elect a government unanimously in favour of the new law. It will avail you nothing. Only a simple majority in the Commission together with a qualified majority in the Council can create new legislation. If a law from Brussels contradicts a law from Westminster, the British law has to yield according to the principle of primacy of community law. This is common knowledge in any academic book, but is not so well known to most MPs and journalists in member states. It shows that democracy-at-a-distance is very difficult, if not impossible, in practice.

European federalists and the majority in the European Parliament acknowledge this criticism of the 'democratic deficit' and propose instead a genuine European democracy modelled on the American Congress. In this way European legislation would have to be negotiated and voted upon in public in two chambers representing the people of Europe and the states of Europe. This is democracy on paper, but since it would be very difficult to get people to vote, it cannot be called a living democracy. In the UK a mere 24 per cent voted at the last European election in 1999. In the 1997 general election in the UK 71 per cent of the electorate turned out.

Supranational European democracy might be a beautiful dream. But we are not engaged in a social sciences project. The attainment of true pan-European democracy requires more than goodwill and high ideals. It would require genetic modification of the European peoples. Quite simply, a true European democracy can exist only if there is a homogeneous European people with identical needs and aspirations.

Once this is accepted, there are only two alternatives. We can accept the diminution and eventual death of democracy in Europe, or keep real democracy at home and turn to Brussels only for those decisions that cannot effectively be managed at national level.

Pollution of the sea and the air transcends national sovereignty. Taxation of multinational companies is difficult unless you have mutual minimum taxation throughout the industrialized world. The battle against climate change cannot be fought from Westminster alone. There are areas where we actually gain genuine influence by cooperating with others. This is not, however, an argument for giving up the main part of our democracy. My advice to all Europeans would be to maintain as much democracy as possible at the national level and thereby allow national parliaments to control legislation in the EU, WTO, and elsewhere.

If you really want to diminish democracy by adopting the Nice Treaty you should at least do it democratically by asking the people in a referendum the following question: Do you want civil servants and ministers in Brussels to pass laws behind closed doors and, as a consequence thereof, give up the possibility to amend them, even after a new general election in the UK?

More qualified majority procedures will mean less democracy in the UK and in every other member state. This criticism is therefore just as valid in France and Germany. The new method of 'enhanced cooperation' will make it very difficult even for Tony Blair to be at the centre of, and heard by, Europe, because further European integration can now also be decided by the qualified majority procedure (except on defence matters). This method makes it possible for France and Germany and their federalist friends to integrate further even if both the UK and the two Scandinavian countries are opposed. Today, 26 votes (out of 87) are needed to block a decision, but the three countries have only 17 votes altogether.

Why should Schröder and Chirac listen to Blair if, from now on, they can continue their process of integration by holding the necessary votes to do so without the consent of the UK? 'Enhanced cooperation' will put the UK at the periphery without the ability to influence the politics — and without the possibility of leaving the EU, because a unanimous decision is needed if a country wants to leave.

There might be a difference between a small state like Denmark and a big nation such as the UK. It is not for me to tell you — the people of the UK — whether to stay and try to influence the EU or to leave the Union entirely, but please do not diminish democracy. We will all be weakened by acceptance of the Nice Treaty.

Denmark initially blocked the Maastricht Treaty in 1992, but this was later overturned. Denmark also voted 'no' to the euro last September in spite of recommendations from all the newspapers except two, all the radio and television channels, 80 per cent of MPs, the Confederation of Trade Unions and most trade unions, 97 per cent of the delegates at the annual Social Democratic Party conference, and 100 per cent of business organizations.

Now the Danish government will not grant the Danes their constitutional right to vote for or against the Nice Treaty. It is therefore up to the UK to block this further erosion of democracy. Do not underestimate this new treaty. It also introduces the qualified majority procedure when it comes to choosing the Commission president and the team of commissioners. The UK once vetoed the superfederalist prime minister of Belgium Jean-Luc Dehaene as Commission president. Next time, via the qualified majority procedure, the EU could veto the choice of Tony Blair or William Hague!

There will be a British citizen in the Commission, but he or she will represent the qualified majority procedure, not Westminster or the British people. The British members of the European Parliament will be paid by Brussels and probably taxed from Brussels as well, and they will be turned into EU representatives to the UK instead of the UK's representatives to Europe.

The Nice Treaty will also be followed by a constitutional process to include the EU Charter of Fundamental Rights in an EU constitution. By 2004 the UK will then have her first written constitution! The UK as a state in a European federation—is this the route you wish to take?

The Nice Treaty is in fact a singularly nasty treaty for democracy in Europe. In the European Parliament we have a group called SOS Democracy, with members from all the different political groups and member states. We have different political positions but agree on a lot of issues as a basis for a European democracy movement. These include:

- The Nice Treaty must not be ratified but instead rene-gotiated.
- The future 'fundamental treaty' must not be a constitution for a European federation, but an international treaty respecting the parliamentary democracies and the national sovereignty of the member states, including a recognized right to leave the EU and clear rules for this.
- The treaty must include a catalogue of competences and explicitly state that competence to legislate resides in national parliaments unless the treaty gives this right, in a specified and clearly well-defined area, to the European institutions.
- The competences at EU level must be limited to trade, common minimum rules for the environment and consumer protection, and such concrete measures as cannot be properly implemented at member state level

because of the international nature of the problem or the demonstrable extra value added through cooperation.

- Future treaties must be put up for legally binding referendums in all countries where the national constitution allows this.

The institutions in Brussels and our representatives abroad must represent us, the electorates of Europe. We should all be the masters of our common future, in cooperation and in friendship, in solidarity with the people of the applicant countries whom we would like to welcome in a slimmer, freer, more democratic and open Europe. Let us unite for proper cooperation between the democracies of Europe.

BECOMING A RELIABLE
TEAM PLAYER
Marta Dassù and Antonio Missiroli

In a long article published in *Le Monde* last year ('Un coeur fort pour l'Europe', 25 May 2000), at the climax of the Fischer–Chirac debate on 'Quo Vadis Europa?', the Italian prime minister, Giuliano Amato, pointedly wondered 'Quo Vadis Britannia?' — because, he wrote, without Great Britain the desirable 'centre of gravity' of the Union would certainly be more compact and homogeneous, but also weaker politically, financially, and militarily, and poorer culturally.

His argument reflects fairly well the prevailing attitude of Italian (and perhaps not only Italian) European-minded elites since the policy change enacted by Tony Blair in 1998. Before that, and especially during the Thatcher years, Italy and Britain had found themselves more often than not at the opposite ends of the euroscepticism/euroenthusiasm spectrum. The procedural tricks that the Italian chair put in place against Margaret Thatcher's obstructive attitude at the European Councils in Milan (1985) and, above all, in Rome (1990) are almost proverbial. More recently, the UK boycott of EU ministerial business in the spring of 1996, in the wake of the ban on British beef generated by the BSE crisis, seriously hampered the Italian presidency of the Union.

And it is no secret that the two countries have adopted opposite views and policies vis-à-vis monetary union, with Italy desperately keen on meeting the convergence criteria set at Maastricht in order to benefit fully from the euro and to participate in what was (and still is) perceived as an eminently political project—and Britain waiting in the wings with a mix of scepticism and worry.

This said, there has also always been potential for bilateral agreement, however occasional, on security and defence matters—leaving aside the fact that Rome has always been in favour (even in the 1960s, in opposition to France's vetoes) of London's full participation in the European integration process. The latent Italo-British entente surfaced in particular in the early 1990s. In October 1991— on the eve of an informal meeting of EU foreign ministers in the run-up to the final Maastricht negotiations— Douglas Hurd and Gianni de Michelis issued a joint declaration that defined the western EU as the European pillar of NATO and proposed the creation of a WEU Rapid Reaction Force. By doing that, they partially responded to parallel Franco-German endeavours (the Eurocorps) and made sure that fledgling European defence efforts would be linked up to NATO, as much in practice as in the treaty language itself.

Ever since, London and Rome have frequently found themselves on the same side of the argument with regard, for instance, to the way in which the EU's Common Foreign and Security Policy (CFSP) framework could be opened up to include applicant countries. At the same time, however, they have differed sharply on how to deal with so-called 'rogue' states and, most notably, on the protracted bombing of Iraq since 1998.

It can come as no surprise therefore if, after the difficult years of John Major's second term in office and of Italy's domestic crisis, Tony Blair's initiative on European defence revived hopes of political convergence both in general (with Britain back 'at the heart of Europe') and in particular (with Britain engaged in giving a credible military dimension to CFSP). Of course, the fact that both governments presented themselves as 'left-of-centre' helped, as did the temporary predominance of coalitions of the same colour all across the EU and—although much more indirectly—the first symptoms of misfiring in the Franco-German 'engine'.

Yet the joint Italian–British declaration on European defence capability, issued in London in July 1999, genuinely translated into practice the combination of old and new common interests—including in the field of the defence industry—that has come to characterize bilateral relations. In it, Italy committed itself to spending more and more effectively on defence and acknowledged the importance of putting in place adequate forces and assets. In return, Britain accepted the logic, and even the language, of 'convergence' as applied to the fledgling European Security and Defence Policy (ESDP) and confirmed its commitment to the institutional framework agreed by the EU in Cologne.

Even beyond that, however, Rome and London have found themselves less at odds than in the past over EU issues, to the extent that Tony Blair was one of the warmest supporters of Romano Prodi's appointment as President of the European Commission. The UK government's drive towards a more flexible and e-compatible economy, which heavily contributed to the success of the Lisbon European Council in March 2000, was strongly supported by both Massimo D'Alema and Giuliano Amato. Britain's insistence on giving more voice to EU citizens and more weight to their national parliaments in European decisions has usually been met with interest in Italy.

Finally, there is enlargement, on whose desirability and urgency the two countries were at loggerheads only a few years ago. London admittedly keeps giving it priority over deepening, but has gradually recognized that internal EU reform is a necessary prerequisite for widening and reuniting Europe. Tony Blair's recent speech in Warsaw represented in fact a remarkable contribution to a common vision of an enlarged but also stronger Union. Rome, in turn, has come to realize that the prospect of enlargement is a powerful tool to enforce further integration and also to match its political and economic interests: after all, Italy is the EU's second biggest investor and trade partner in the applicant countries after Germany.

On other issues, however, the two countries remain distant: in particular, the final outcome of the Inter-Governmental Conference (IGC) at Nice has shown the extent to which British and Italian positions on Europe still differ, much as the divergence was probably made wider by tactical considerations. On taxation — whether or not to resort to qualified majority voting on fiscal policies — the divide seems deepest. At bottom, however, it all comes down to the basic decision on economic and monetary union: if, in other words, the pound joins the euro, the issue will be settled jointly; if not, it will be settled inside the eurozone and Britain will have to respond from outside.

On most institutional matters on the IGC agenda the British negotiating stance seemed dictated more by domestic concerns — the threat of a eurosceptic offensive against 'selling out' national sovereignty — than by a vision fundamentally hostile to European integration per se. Even in the one policy area where the UK could easily claim a leadership role, namely ESDP proper, British negotiators were extremely timid and wary. The little change that was eventually inserted into the treaties simply to update their wording was brought about at the initiative of a smaller (and no less Atlanticist) partner, namely the Netherlands, with Italian and Belgian support. Tony Blair himself dropped at the last minute the already limited idea of applying 'enhanced cooperation' to defence in general — one of the domains where it would make most sense — and even to the defence industry specifically (thus slowing down or even damaging processes, already under way, in which Britain is a leading player), mainly out of fear of an all-out Conservative campaign against the alleged 'Euro-Army'.

As seen from Italy, therefore, there are still limits to the consistency and so the credibility of Britain's rapprochement to the political 'heart' of the EU. Such limits—in spite of Robin Cook's recent groundbreaking remarks on British and European 'patriotism'—risk strengthening the hand of those who think that Britain's policy change is just a smoke-screen and that instead it is in Italy's best interest to focus exclusively on the original 'heart' of the Union, the six founding members of the Community.

All this said, it is curious to note—especially from an Italian perspective—how far (and unexpectedly) radically eurosceptic and federalist views of EU integration converge in their almost caricatured reading of the process as a zero-sum game, a neat transfer of 'sovereignty' from a nineteenth-century-type nation-state to some 'supranational', technocratic Leviathan: a transfer feared and opposed by British eurosceptics, hailed and advocated by Italian ultra-federalists, who see in it rescue and redemption from old national shortcomings. Instead, all evidence shows that European integration is a much more complex game in which transfers do happen, of course, but what move and change are the loci and the modalities in which national 'sovereignty' (or rather what is left of it) is exercised. In fact, the real transition is not from nation-state to superstate—or superpower, for that matter—but from nation-state to member state.

The EU is about sharing not about relinquishing 'sovereignty', and it is in essence a positive-sum game: in security as well as in trade and other matters, one is tempted to say, *l'Union fait la force*. For as long as European integration is not seen and presented like that, with all the challenges and opportunities related to such a vision, Italy will probably keep having problems with its internal capacity and motivation to modernize, thus punching well below its weight. Britain, in turn, will keep being haunted by the imperative to win 'game, set, and match' against (rather than play with) its European partners and therefore not be considered by them a fully reliable team player.

12 THE VIEW FROM AMERICA

Many eurosceptics see British involvement in European integration as a threat to the famed 'special relationship' between Britain and the US. Some believe a better national direction would be a deepening of the British bond with North America through Britain joining the North American Free Trade Association (NAFTA), which currently consists of the US, Canada, and Mexico.

For Tony Blair any attempt to counterpose Europe and America is a false choice. The metaphor he likes is the one which speaks of Britain as a 'bridge' between the two continents. These divisions are paralleled in North America, where there are different views on the path along which Britain's national interest lies.

HOW TO REMAIN AMERICA'S PRIVILEGED PARTNER

Philip Gordon

The American interest in the UK's European policy can be stated in a fairly simple syllogism. The first premise is that the US has a strong interest in an integrated, enlarged EU based on free-market principles and active in the wider world. Such a Union will help ensure peace on the European continent (where America fought several costly wars during the twentieth century), provide the basis for prosperity in a bloc of nearly 500 million people (which is America's leading trading and investment partner), and contribute to security and development in Eurasia and in the wider world (in ways that none of America's other global partners are willing or able to do).

The second premise is that the EU is much more likely to evolve in this direction if the UK is an active, influential actor within it than if London is marginalized or excluded. Even as its political, economic, and strategic orientations gradually align with those of continental Europe, the UK maintains the broadly liberal, Atlanticist, and internationalist views that the US wants to see shape the European agenda.

Thus the conclusion: the American interest is in a UK that plays an influential role from within the EU rather than one that stands aside, let alone one that seeks to scupper the EU project altogether. We would rather see a Britain that helps to ensure that the Union remains an open, outward-looking, cooperative partner of the US than a Britain that joins us in splendid isolation and exclusion.

Of course in real life the choices are rarely so simple. The UK's dilemma for the past 50 years has been whether or not to participate in European initiatives that it does not fully support. Participating means boarding a train whose destination may not be Britain's preferred one, but failing to participate means losing the chance to influence the choice of that destination, and allowing the train to go there without it.

In practice, as Hugo Young so compellingly demonstrated in his book *This Blessed Plot*, the pattern has most often been that the UK initially stays out but eventually decides to get in, once it becomes clear that the project is going to go forward. This was true for the Coal and Steel Community in 1952, the European Economic Community in 1959, various defence initiatives in the 1970s and 1980s, Schengen in the 1990s, and now—potentially at least—for the euro. The cost of this approach for Britain has been an inability to shape many of the initiatives that it has failed to prevent and persistent scepticism in Europe about the UK's commitment to the European project.

The dilemmas for the US have been similar, and so has the American response, at least since the 1960s. Whenever Europe undertakes any new initiative, the initial American reaction tends to be a combination of scepticism and nervousness: Will a European Common Market be protectionist? Will the single market programme lead to a 'Fortress Europe'? Will a common European foreign and security policy undermine NATO? Will the euro threaten the dollar? Thus the American dilemma toward Britain's European policy is similar to Britain's toward Europe: Do we want the UK to stay out and help prevent the project from taking off, or do we want it to join and help shape it? Given that all of these initiatives have ultimately been implemented in one way or another despite American and British scepticism, the answer should now be as obvious to the US as it is to the UK: our common interest is in a Britain that can shape European initiatives from the start rather than one that either has no say or that seeks but fails to prevent them.

To see why, consider all the key areas of the European debate, and ask whether Europe is better for America with the British playing an influential inside role or whether it would be better if the UK were left out. (My assumption here, backed by the 50 years of evidence already mentioned, is that British abstinence will not be enough to prevent the other Europeans from eventually moving forward.)

One reason we want to see an influential Britain in the EU is as a hedge against the Union moving in an elitist, federalist direction that would make it less, rather than more, democratic, and arguably more subject to public backlash. To be sure, a federal model would be more efficient in theory, but just as majorities in most EU countries now support the Union, similar majorities oppose centralization in Brussels, which London is certain to help prevent. Even a continental federalist like Jacques Delors once admitted that 'you have to keep the British in the EC for their democratic tradition if nothing else'.

The outcome of the December 2000 Nice summit—which reinforced the inter-governmental character of the Union—was certainly not pretty, but it did reflect the reality that the EU is still made up of separate, democratic nation-states, whose rights and interests must be protected. The summit's adoption of the principle of 'enhanced cooperation' is a much more pragmatic, workable arrangement than would be the adoption of a formalized, federal 'hard core' from which the British would be left out.

Britain's support for EU enlargement is also in the American interest in projecting stability and security across the continent. Many Americans, of course, all too glibly call on Europeans to generously extend their borders to the east in a way we would never consider doing for Mexico (or even Canada), but more than a decade after the end of the Cold War it is time to accelerate the process. Tony Blair's October 2000 speech in Warsaw, calling on the Union to enlarge to include at least several new countries by the 2004 parliamentary elections, was a constructive contribution to the European debate. Achieving this goal would be a historic achievement.

A third way in which an influential Britain helps shape Europe in the right way is through its promotion of economic openness. The UK's traditional free-trade instincts and the Labour Party's more recent adoption of pragmatic liberalism work both to promote prosperity and to keep the Union open to the economic interaction with the US that is so vital to both sides of the Atlantic. Calls by some British eurosceptics for the UK to join NAFTA are not only unrealistic but also a poor alternative to open trade and investment between the US and the EU, which a strong UK voice in Europe can help promote. British activism from the inside was a critical component in the success of the '1992' single market programme, essential in the June 2000 Lisbon 'dotcom' summit, and the only hope for reform of the Common Agricultural Policy. This influence helps to ensure the sort of modern, prosperous Europe in which entrepreneurship, trade, and investment can flourish.

The US also has a strong interest in an effective European Security and Defence Policy (ESDP) compatible with NATO, and this cannot be achieved without British participation and influence. To the extent that ESDP leads to greater actual European military capabilities—not at all a certainty but a reasonable hope—it contributes to burden-sharing within the Atlantic Alliance. An effective ESDP is also in the US interest as a possible alternative to NATO in places 'where the Alliance as a whole is not engaged', to borrow the agreed language of NATO and EU communiqués. Many US senators are inherently sceptical about anything that could undermine NATO's pre-eminence, but nothing would make those same senators happier than the thought that Europe could effect more military intervention in Africa or Asia, sparing the US the burden of having to do so. Finally, America has an interest in an effective European military capability to deal even with contingencies in Europe, like the Balkans, if the US proves unwilling to play its part.

ESDP is only in the US interest, however, if it is done in ways that neither threaten NATO's effectiveness nor lead to the costly and unnecessary duplication of all too limited means. The UK has over the past two years played an indispensable role in ensuring that these risks are avoided, which would not have been possible had London not been intimately involved.

Obviously, the defining issue regarding the British relationship with Europe will be its decision on whether or not to join the euro. This is of course a decision only the British can make, and the US has no particular stake in the abstract. If the British public is strongly opposed and the UK business cycle is significantly out of sync with Europe's, then the UK should stay out; in the short run this will do little harm. Ultimately, however, a successful single currency helping to facilitate cross-border trade and investment, control inflation, and lower interest rates across the entire European single market would be good for both the UK and the US.

For years, American economists were generally dubious about the merits of a single European currency on economic grounds, but they were also sceptical that it would ever happen and they were wrong about that. To the basic economic argument that a single currency will not work in Europe because European wages, prices, and labour markets are not flexible enough there is an equally basic response: they must be made more flexible. This is not only a good thing in its own right, but it is far more likely to happen if the UK is part of the eurozone than if it is not. For better or worse, the euro now exists, and it is hard to see how anyone has an interest in its failure. Just as the British eventually reconciled themselves to the need to participate in the Common Market they once opposed, this is a reality that London will ultimately need to accept.

Aside from all the potential benefits to both Britain and America of a strong British role in the EU, it is also worth mentioning the possible risks of the alternative. For the past ten years, Britain's 'special relationship' with the US has proven more enduring than many had predicted when the Cold War ended. London (and Paris) still garner more attention in Washington than Brussels—and even than Berlin, which was tipped at the time as America's new 'partner in leadership'. But Britain's privileged position is not guaranteed, and it is far more vulnerable on the outskirts of Europe than it would be at Europe's core.

As European integration proceeds (and succeeds) in the economic, diplomatic, and military domains—and as

Philip Gordon

Germany continues to overcome the costs of unification and its inhibitions about playing a geopolitical role—the US will inevitably have to cast its sights more toward the continent than toward the UK. Fully in Europe, Britain has every chance to remain America's preferred and privileged partner. Marginalized from the EU, Britain could find itself less influential in Washington as well. It is time for Britain, to put a new spin on Churchill's phrase, to be 'of' Europe, as well as 'for' it.

THE ATLANTIC COMMUNITY

Conrad Black

Since the Eisenhower era the US has been urging Britain into Europe, initially to strengthen the resolve of the Europeans as cold warriors and more recently out of habit and to be a force for good government in Europe. These motives are understandable, but have nothing to do with the national interest of the UK and no longer accord with the national interest of the US.

The US foreign policy establishment, including most foreign and security experts in the new administration, are increasingly suspicious of the motives of the eurofederalists. The chairmen of the Senate Foreign Relations and Banking Committees, Jesse Helms and Phil Gramm, Henry Kissinger, Bush advisors Paul Wolfowitz and Richard Perle, and the new President himself are among those who have expressed interest in breathing new life into the Anglo-American special relationship.

A European foreign and security policy by majority vote, the next step after monetary union, would be the end of any special British relationship with anyone. If such a common foreign and security policy by majority voting had been in effect at the time of the Gulf War in 1990–1, it is almost certain that the majority of EU nations would have voted against military action and 40,000 excellent British servicemen would not have participated. Nor could Britain have bucked the inclinations of her European partners and allowed the Americans to bomb Libya from US bases in Britain in 1986. Nor could Britain have launched and successfully conducted the Falklands campaign with US help in 1981.

It is now almost 40 years since President Truman's secretary of state Dean Acheson said 'Britain has lost an empire but not yet found a role'. Successive US administrations have been aware of how difficult this task has been and still is. The American foreign policy community has not failed to notice that Britain is regularly rebuffed in a more cavalier manner by Europe, and especially France, than has occurred in Anglo-American relations since Suez.

Washington is now beginning to perceive that euro-integrationists (usually) unwittingly threaten the dissolution of the Atlantic alliance. Some of the more influential euro-advocates seem to seek to reconfigure the alliance on lines that are unlikely to be acceptable to the US. Like a great St Bernard, the US will provide the muscle while Europe holds the leash and gives the orders. Even those in Britain who wanted to deny the US the right to attack Libya from US bases in Britain in 1986 believed the US should continue to have the privilege of guaranteeing Western European security.

During the Cold War the perceived greater European risk because of the proximity of the USSR was assumed to off-set the greater American defence burden. Now that that risk has virtually disappeared, there is neither the need nor inclination in Europe to increase the burden. And it is hard on the basis of events unfolding almost weekly not to think that any move to do so is more likely to be motivated by a desire to be a rival, rather than a stronger ally, for the US.

The US has long been irritated by the European habit of trying to fashion a mid-East policy by awaiting American initiatives and then staking out positions more favourable to the Arab powers. This has contributed nothing useful to the peace process and it is likely to become more trouble-some.

The US government is also concerned that the EU's shabby, arms' length treatment of Turkey will destabilize that crucial country and the entire region, though there has been some relative moderation lately. In this policy field, Britain's commendable dissent has been gratefully noted.

The European practice of embracing the Turks whenever they need an ally in the Middle East and then spurning them as a rabble of Islamic migrants whenever they seek a closer association with Europe is in vivid contrast to the wholehearted generosity of the American and Canadian extension of their free trade agreement to Mexico, and of US assistance during Mexico's currency crises. This pol-icy has contributed indispensably to massive economic and commercial reform and full democratization in Mexico.

Even if there is only a possibility that a federal Europe could be in some measure a nuisance to the US, American interests would be well served by keeping so comparatively important a country as Britain at least as close to the US as to an integrated Europe, and offering it an alternative most Britons would welcome to absorption in an uncertainly motivated Europe.

Over a wide range of matters, including trade, the US should and soon will decide whether it wants the UK to continue as its deputy sheriff or to barricade itself into Europe, wherever that may lead. And it should make its wishes known to the British, obviously without offending the continental Europeans. The evident alternative is to energize and rename NAFTA and open it to all economically and politically compatible states. There are already such discussions with Chile, Singapore, Norway, and Switzerland. In the opinion of a growing number of influential Americans, an invitation should be extended to the UK.

It is obvious to observers, including Americans, that British trade patterns are also clearly distinguishable from those of the other EU countries. Almost twice as much of Britain's trade, as a percentage, is with North America than is the case with other EU countries as a group, and it is rising more quickly than British trade with the EU. Britain's share of trade with the EU has actually declined recently. Conversely, the exports of a number of countries to the EU, including those of the US, have risen considerably more rapidly than have Britain's in recent years. Over the last ten years direct net investment in the UK from the US and Canada has been one and a half times the corresponding figure for EU investment in Britain. And British net direct investment in North America has been more than double UK investment in the EU. These trends are continuing, impervious to EU preferences.

Now that the World Trade Organization is administering the Uruguay Round of trade liberalization agreements, the EU's common external tariff has fallen from 5.7 per cent to 3.6 per cent. The fear of being frozen out of Europe by vindictive community bureaucrats is still invoked by British euro-advocates, but is now seen by almost everyone outside the British government as a complete fraud. Almost no one and certainly no credible American proposes that Britain withdraw altogether from Europe, including the common market. Some British eurofanatics claim that Europe could not allow Britain to stay in the common market if it withdrew from the EU, even though Norway, Iceland, Liechtenstein, Switzerland, in many respects Israel, and even Mexico enjoy that status. They also claim NAFTA wouldn't have Britain.

In fact, Britain could surely use the existence of its veto right and its large current account deficit with the EU, supplemented by an easily obtainable NAFTA invitation, to negotiate complete reciprocal access of goods and people and withdrawal from the EU political and judicial institutions. This would emancipate Britain from the mass of authoritarian Euro-directives with which it has been deluged. And as Senator Gramm said in London last spring, if Britain wanted an invitation to join NAFTA, it would be issued at once.

Such an initiative would actually be complementary to the current EU expansion of its trade association agreements, the unprecedented pursuit of regional trade agreements by Japan, and the ambitious activities of Mexico with Japan, Latin America, and the EU. American trade experts are coming to believe that an expanding NAFTA would have every commercial advantage over the EU. It is based on the American free market which has created (net) an average of two million more new jobs per year in the US and Canada than has the EU for the last 15 years. The US will not make any significant concessions of sovereignty and does not expect other countries to do so either.

Such a bloc could, if it chose to do so, expand through South America and into Eastern Europe faster than the EU, encumbered as the EU is by the Common Agricultural Policy and a powerful urge to protect onerous French and German social costs.

Britain's chances of evangelizing the Europeans in favour of transparency, privatization, deregulation, lower taxes, and labour flexibility and efficiency are unclear, but would be much greater as a NAFTA vanguard than as a component of an integrated social democratic Europe.

Washington is steadily reminded of the extent to which eurofederalism is inspired by a resentment of the soft hegemony of the Americans and, as some Europeans would have it, the Anglo-Americans, these fifty years. When scratched at all, many of the leading eurofederalists profess some resentment at the subordination of Europe during the Cold War and have a somewhat mystical concept of the early re-emergence of European leadership in the world. American policy-makers of both parties are well aware that Europe possesses neither the geopolitical strength nor, except for the British, the political maturity to exercise any such role.

The main home for such sentiments remains France, where they are espoused by both pro- and anti-European forces. Thus, François Mitterrand is recorded by Georges-Marc Benamou in *Le Dernier Mitterrand* as saying: 'France does not know it, but we are at war with America. Yes, a permanent war, a vital war, an economic war, a war without death. Yes, they are very hard the Americans, they are voracious, they want undivided power over the world.'

The French foreign minister, Hubert Védrine, has described the new NATO members as US Trojan horses, and has made an endless series of inflammatory comments about the US, including exhortations to 'stand up to' the US over Iraq. This is not the conduct of a reliable ally, and President Chirac's implausible claim that the European defence force is the beginning of the 'projection of European power throughout the globe' is more of the same. Militarily it is nonsense, but the spirit behind such an assertion is not a supportive aspiration to alliance co-leadership, but mere mischief-making. These comments have resonated very poorly in Washington, as has Europe's overwhelming preference for Gore in the recent election, especially prime minister Jospin's outrageous questioning of the legitimacy of the result.

Britain is at the centre, geographically, culturally, and politically, of an Atlantic community; whereas she is in all respects on the periphery of an exclusively or predominantly European order. The unintended consequence of a Britain ever more closely integrated into a European foreign and defence policy would be a Britain torn away from her natural Atlanticist vocation and a US largely deprived of her principal ally. In the US as in Britain, it is asked with increasing frequency why either country should seek this. The question now is whether in the next four years, Britain will ask to join NAFTA or be invited without asking. If Britain played her hand astutely, it could soon be courted by Europe and the Americans instead of being treated cavalierly by Brussels and with benign detachment by Washington.

Britain's relationships with both Europe and the US are special and should remain so. The alternatives are to languish in an isolation that would reduce the UK to an inflated Switzerland or to be subsumed into Europe like an expanded Netherlands. Britain's destiny, American observers believe, is, like its history, more exalted than that.

13 SHOULD WE STAY OR SHOULD WE GO?

On 1 January 1973 the Union Jack was hoisted outside the Brussels headquarters of what was then called the European Economic Community or Common Market, as under the prime ministership of Edward Heath the UK became a member state. In 1974 Heath was defeated by Harold Wilson, whose Labour government was pledged to seek a renegotiation of the terms of entry, which it would then put to the people. The new terms (which were not really that different from the old terms) were approved in a referendum in June 1975 by 67 per cent to 33 per cent. This was despite the fact that six months earlier polls had shown a majority in favour of withdrawal. The vote followed a campaign in which the balance of mainstream political forces—leading and popular politicians, the media, and business—was predominantly pro-EEC.

For the pro-Europeans this was the issue settled. For some of those who wanted out, it was only a brief pause in their campaign for withdrawal. As John Curtice shows, they currently enjoy significant public support which has been growing over the past decade. Although very few politicians in the main parties explicitly back leaving the EU, this point of view has found political expression in the United Kingdom Independence Party. In the 1999 European Parliament elections UKIP took 7 per cent of the vote and won three seats.

FROM THE WISTFUL TO THE INEVITABLE

Nigel Farage

It was only a few years ago that, in the aftermath of the Maastricht Treaty, a few of us resolved that the principal political parties were by and large pursuing an agenda set by their leaders' interests and ideals rather than by their members, and that a new party was therefore needed to campaign for Britain's withdrawal from the EU.

At the time this notion, if popular amongst the wistful and romantic, was considered eccentric by the mass and unthinkable by the urban, *soi-disant* intellectuals who controlled the media. In retrospect, however, the unthinkable seems to have become inevitable. That urban elite has not shifted its position and the political classes have continued to insist that Britain's future is inextricable from their own ambitions. But, without benefit, then, of media encouragement or political leadership, more than 50 per cent of the British people have, quite simply, had enough and believe that we would be better off out.

Although the politicians of the 1970s who led us into Europe were well aware of the constitutional consequences, they deliberately and cynically advanced only economic arguments for entry into what, we were then told, was merely a 'common market' and wilfully concealed from the electorate the political and legal costs. At that time, the economic argument seemed overwhelming. The British economy appeared to be in permanent decline. The opportunity to hitch our wagon to the ever-rising German star was irresistible. Trade, it was reasoned, would boom, and all participants in such a free trade area would benefit.

Twenty-eight years on, we can appraise the true economic consequences of membership. Certainly the volume of trade with other member states has grown, but the balance — or grotesque imbalance — of that trade has been injurious, with the UK having traded at a deficit of a staggering £175 billion. Add to this the loss of our fishing and farming industries and the unknown but undoubtedly vast cost of implementing some 30,000 new laws at the EU's command, and any putative benefit is annihilated. Further add to this the membership fee to this club, currently running at £11.5 billion a year, with which we subsidize our direct competitors, and the overall cost has been overwhelming.

The EU and its apologists like to think of themselves as modern, even futuristic, visionaries. In fact, the whole idea is quaintly, even rather sweetly, old-fashioned.

Economically, the case that membership of the EU enlarges the home market by lowering tariff barriers is outdated. Immediately after the war tariffs, often in excess of 30 per cent, were imposed upon manufactured goods in the western world. Since then, GATT and the WTO have characterized a continuous process of trade liberalization. Tariff barriers on manufactured goods are now down to a maximum of 3.6 per cent. Once outside the EU, it will be a straightforward business to renegotiate a genuine free trade agreement. The other European nations need the UK market considerably more than we need them. Already non-EU states such as Norway and Switzerland have free trade deals with the EU. Even Mexico, a member of NAFTA, has contrived to negotiate such a deal.

Assertions that three million British jobs depend upon our membership of the EU are therefore arbitrary, absurd scaremongering, and ignore the fact that the UK is the largest single market for the EU. I have yet to hear it suggested by even the most ardent europhile that BMW, Renault, Fiat, Braun, or other European giants will continue to trade with Mexico, but will cease to trade with the UK should we leave the political club.

Politically, the European project is equally old-fashioned. The notion of artificial amalgams or Soviets of states has been wholly discredited, with every such construct disintegrating into its constituent parts, often amidst bloodshed. When people realize that their votes change nothing, that their regional or cultural interests are disregarded, and that true democratic process has been hijacked by distant, self-interested, self-important, and self-perpetuating bureaucracy, there is an imperative —

some would say a duty — to resort to civil disobedience simply in order to be heard. At the last, by one means or another, they will be heard. We pray that it will be sooner and peaceably, rather than later and bloodily.

Where, after the war, some 50 nations sat in the United Nations, there are now over 190, as around the globe peoples demand democratic self-determination. The principal prerequisite of democratic self-determination is the right to elect and, perhaps more important, to remove from office the representatives of diverse regions and interests.

The EU is not a democratic institution. No directive or regulation originates in the Parliament or with the petition of a constituent. Every one is initiated and imposed by the unelected European Commission, whilst interest rates, whether appropriate or not, are decided by the appointed functionaries of the European Central Bank. Yes, there is a 'Parliament', but MEPs are quite literally powerless, and speaking, which gives parliament its name and is generally considered essential to debate, is a valueless currency in the European Parliament. The average length of a speech is two minutes. When the time is up, the microphone is simply and unceremoniously switched off. Rhetoric and conviction, even facts and figures, alter nothing. Nobody listens. We are going through a procedure, a charade, calculated to afford the process a spurious democratic legitimacy.

And we are bribed to continue the charade. So long as we press the 'Yes', 'No', and 'Abstain' buttons frequently enough, we draw our generous allowances. Should we fail to do so, those allowances can be cut by up to 50 per cent. The Parliament, furthermore, never stands down. New members find themselves voting on second readings of bills which their predecessors initiated. Nothing must stop the endless sausage-factory of regulations to interfere in every aspect of our lives.

British governments may frequently be unpopular, but, in the past at least, they could claim legitimacy. We in the EU Parliament can make no such claim. The Parliament rarely has the temerity to question draft legislation handed down by the unelected Commission, and, when it does, it is only in matters of detail. Above all, perhaps, the Parliament has never questioned the all-important need for particular legislation. To do so would be to question the value of its function and its very existence.

Power without responsibility, 'the prerogative of the harlot', is now the prerogative too of UK governments. Again and again our ministers return to our shores with the plaint, 'We did our best, but our hands were tied,' an admission which would have made their predecessors weep for shame. How can a directly elected government have its hands tied in doing what it was elected to do — governing the country in the best interests of the electorate? The entire process of suing for the return of our funds and pleading for favours from the EU is an undignified one. The divorce, when it comes, will be a liberating experience, restoring self-confidence and the responsibility which freedom engenders.

The UK now has the fourth largest economy in the world. We are the largest foreign investor in the USA and the only EU country which can claim to be a global trading nation. Europhiles prefer to ignore these facts and to disparage at once our international status and our ability to govern ourselves freely and independently in a free world.

The 1975 referendum which endorsed our entry to the 'Common Market' took place when inflation was at its 27 per cent peak and industry was in disarray. Now, following the necessary reforms of the 1980s and the growth in global trade, we have no need to be inextricably bound to our next door neighbours in a bloc which restricts autonomy, subsumes cultures, diminishes responsibility, and threatens world peace. We have made the experiment—or rather, the politicians have made it, with us mere duped guinea pigs. It has proved a failure. We would be better off out.

RESTATING THE CASE
Nick Clegg

The EU is over-centralized, strangled by red tape, protectionist, unlimited in its appetite for new powers, led by mandarins answerable to nobody, and governed by inefficient and endemically corrupt institutions.

This is a widely held view of the EU in the UK. If this characterization were even half accurate, I hope I would be the first to man the barricades of a worthy anti-European revolt. But the reality is very different. And also a great deal more mundane.

Far from being a disembodied entity capable of overturning centuries of tradition and independence with the stroke of a legislative pen, it is a complex, largely inter-governmental, experiment in supranational integration with clearly circumscribed powers. Whilst the EU has some trappings of a federal order—notably the pre-eminence of European law and the European Commission's autonomy—it remains an undertaking limited by the ambitions granted to it by national governments.

And it is premised on a breathtakingly simple insight: that in a world in which economic, environmental, and even political forces are increasingly footloose, governments are only able to assert some measure of authority over the conditions which determine the prosperity and security of their citizens if they pool sovereignty in those areas in which it is no longer feasible to govern alone.

Trade, competition, monetary policy, environmental and consumer protection, asylum and immigration, defence and security are all areas of public life in which the authority and reach of the nineteenth-century nation-state has been found to be desperately wanting. Far from inhibiting the exercise of sovereignty, the EU allows its member states to extend sovereignty over areas which they could not possibly influence on their own.

Unwittingly, then, the European project launched in 1957 as an act of post-war economic and political reconciliation is proving to be a highly sophisticated response to the new problem of diminished national sovereignty brought about by globalization. This is perhaps its most enduring contemporary rationale.

It is telling that, at a time when nations everywhere are facing similar global challenges, calls to emulate the EU are growing louder in Asia, Africa, and Latin America. It is equally telling that all the countries of Central and Eastern Europe, without exception, which had fallen under the yoke of Soviet Communism, recognize that their vocation as modern European democracies cannot be secured without EU membership. It would be perverse in the extreme for the UK to turn its back on a club at a time when so many others are beating at its doors.

So why is the question of the UK's continued membership of the EU once again on the political agenda? Almost unique in the EU, the UK has a considerable body of press and political opinion for which Europe has become an abiding, almost obsessive preoccupation. Large parts of the ownership and editorial elite in the written press have been joined by a major political party, the Conservative Party, in attaching numerous conditions to their continued consent to UK membership of the EU which point inevitably towards withdrawal.

So restating the arguments in favour of EU membership has become all the more necessary. Ever since the referendum on UK membership of the European Community was fought in 1975, the leading arguments deployed in favour of EU membership have been economic. They remain as striking as ever: over three million jobs are directly dependent on the UK's membership of the EU; almost 60 per cent of British exports of goods go to the EU, compared to 15 per cent to the US; 49 per cent of total UK trade in services and goods is with the eurozone, compared to 16 per cent with the US; the EU is by far the world's largest single market — it accounts for around one-fifth of world trade in goods and one-quarter of all world trade in services.

Further statistics can be deployed concerning the cost of EU membership: the total EU budget as a proportion of public wealth is barely 1.1 per cent, compared to a total tax take by the UK Treasury of just under 40 per cent of national wealth; the per capita cost to the UK taxpayer of

EU membership is miniscule, and certainly negative when set against the vast commercial advantages which accrue to the UK because of the benefits of the single market.

Yet, somehow, these arguments are insufficient. The massive body of evidence that EU membership contributes directly to our economic prosperity does not seem to make the impression on public opinion which logic suggests it should.

The reason, perhaps, is because the UK entered the European club with a very different psychological disposition towards membership than others: for a nation which had been the most powerful force in world events for most of the nineteenth and early twentieth century, being a member of any European club was bound to be taken as a sign of comparative weakness—a final, painful admission that the UK was no longer able to disregard its dependence on others.

By contrast, for almost all the other members of the European Community, membership held an entirely different significance: for the Germans, French, Italians, and, later, for the Spanish, Portuguese, and Greeks, it was a crowning moment of economic and political maturity. War, occupation, dictatorship, and economic failure were replaced by a collective undertaking to consolidate democracy and successful economic interdependence. They will be joined in the coming years by new members from Central and Eastern Europe with almost identical motivations.

That is why the voices of continental pro-Europeans still tremor with pride when they consider the remarkable political and economic progress brought about by European integration. That is also why the voices of anti-Europeans in Britain still tremor with an angry insecurity. Membership of the EU is a bewildering thing for those who are loath to accept that the relative authority and power of the UK is radically diminished.

Indeed, the fiction of continued British superiority is indispensable to those who seek to justify withdrawal from the EU. As the argument about the UK's role in Europe intensifies, a factually illiterate nationalism is emerging which blithely assumes that the UK outperforms the rest of the EU in most fields.

Thus it is widely held that the UK's economy is performing better than the rest of the EU, when objective indicators of growth, productivity, inflation, interest rates, and even the rate of job creation are now superior in almost all major EU economies. Per capita, the UK is now the sixth poorest nation in the EU. The UK has one of the highest rates of child poverty in the EU (the proportion of children living in real poverty is five times higher than in the Netherlands). It is one of the lowest performers in basic literacy and numeracy levels (21.8 per cent of adults in the UK are functionally illiterate compared to 7.5 per cent in Sweden). Its public services are notoriously poor compared to other EU countries, nowhere more obvious than in public transport. And so on.

Perhaps, then, it is time to restate the case for membership in terms which go well beyond conventional economic and political point scoring. Perhaps it is time to cast EU membership in terms of the kind of society the British aspire towards. Is it not myopic in the extreme to overlook the fact that in the EU some of the most prosperous, dynamic, and highly educated societies have been built in recent years? The stunning development of societies as diverse as Ireland and Spain should give even the most hardened sceptic pause for thought. Is it not self-evidently in the interests of a nation such as the UK, which has experienced almost continual relative decline since the war, to endeavour to learn from such successful neighbours through its EU membership?

In the end, it is no doubt a question of identity. Are we, as opponents of EU membership suggest, to emulate Norway, Switzerland, Hong Kong, or Malaysia — small nations unfettered by wider duties, cut off from wider responsibilities? Are we, as many arch-Atlanticists suggest, to become a satellite state linked to the loose trading arrangements between the USA, Canada, and Mexico — a kind of mid-Atlantic subsidiary of the North American economy?

Or are we to accept that by any interpretation of our geography and history we are a European nation from head to toe. That for a large trading nation with a long tradition of international engagement and influence, our standing in the world is entirely dependent on our standing in Europe. That meaningful sovereignty in the modern world can only be exercised in close conjunction with our neighbours. That building the largest borderless market-place in the world, raising European environmental standards, working together against cross-border crime, ensuring that Europe can enforce peace and stability near its borders, are not luxuries we can ignore. They are, quite simply, indispensable to the future prosperity and security of the UK.

14 PARTY PERSPECTIVES

TAKING THE LEAD IN EUROPE
Keith Vaz

Since Labour entered government in 1997, the UK's approach to Europe has been marked by a willingness to engage positively with partners and find solutions to seemingly intractable problems. But we have done more than this. We have also shown that, contrary to past precedent, the UK can take the lead in Europe, ensuring that the EU and its institutions are prepared for the challenges of the twenty-first century.

Our approach has come as a pleasant surprise to many. After too many years in the wilderness, where our approach to EU negotiations was often characterized by isolation and intransigence, we have finally embraced a simple truth: our destiny lies at the heart of Europe.

There are numerous examples where our constructive approach is bearing fruit. We have played a leading role in moves to strengthen the EU's voice on the international stage. For too long the Union's voice in international affairs has not been commensurate with its economic weight. We are beginning to redress the balance: our proposals to strengthen the EU's foreign and defence policy have been welcomed.

But it is perhaps in the field of European economic reform that our contribution has been clearest. One of the EU's finest achievements has been to create the world's largest single market for trade in goods and services. Down the years, European companies and consumers alike have benefited enormously from the efficiency gains, cheaper products, and price transparency the single market has brought. But, despite all of these achievements, the model is incomplete. And in the twenty-first century, we face enormous challenges if we are to realize the potential of the IT revolution and match the strides the US economy has taken over the past decade. That is why we will continue to play a leading role in discussions to modernize the European economy.

At the historic Lisbon summit in 2000/, EU leaders agreed a blueprint for economic reform that bears many of the hallmarks of the British model. Under the headline commitment, championed by Tony Blair, the EU has set itself the target of becoming the most competitive and dynamic knowledge-based economy in the world by 2010, capable of sustainable economic growth with more and better jobs and greater social cohesion.

The Lisbon agenda means: changing old practices that block higher economic growth and more employment; keeping Europe's values of innovation and social justice; maximizing the benefits of the single market and increasing Europe's competitiveness; and making monetary union succeed—employability, flexibility, and stronger competition, rather than monetary policy, are now the key tools to enable Europe to adjust to unexpected economic events. Lisbon was the first time that the EU set itself a ten-year goal for change, backed up by a mechanism to ensure delivery.

Ensuring that Europe has a flexible and dynamic economy is all the more important when one considers the main challenge facing the Union this decade: the enlargement of the EU to Eastern, Central, and Southern Europe.

The Nice Treaty marked the end of a year-long phase of intensive EU discussions. Nice was a watershed summit and the implications for the UK are enormous. So how will Nice shape the debate on the 'Future of Europe' opened by the prime minister, the German foreign minister, Joschka Fischer, and the French president, Jacques Chirac, last year? I believe that Nice finally nailed the myth that EU member states are bent on creating a federal superstate.

Each country took a clear national agenda to the summit. We were no different. In the White Paper we launched in February 2000, we highlighted the following key objectives that would be central to our agenda:

- to agree a treaty that opened the door for enlargement, and all the associated benefits that would bring;
- to secure more power for the UK through changes to the weighting of votes in the Council of Ministers to reflect better the population of individual countries;

- to agree on a smaller and better Commission;
- to agree more majority voting where this would pro-mote our interests (for example, delivering a more open single market), while keeping our veto where it would protect them (for example, on tax and social security);
- to create a more flexible Europe, by agreeing new arrangements to allow groups of countries to move for-ward in certain areas without requiring all members to do so.

Nice involved some tough choices for all involved, but the prize of enlargement ensured that in the end we found a way through. The treaty we agreed incorporates all of these objectives and more. For example, we now have EU agreement:

- to streamline the European Commission from 2005 — this should ensure faster decision-making and less red tape;
- to boost the UK's influence in the Council of Ministers by reweighting our vote to reflect more accurately the size of our population and to ensure that decision-making in the Council remains democratic — we came home with a substantial increase in our vote (from 10 votes in the Council to 29) and greater weight relative to the small and medium-sized countries;
- to extend qualified majority voting in areas where faster EU decision-making will benefit the UK (for example, in the field of senior appointments and international trade);
- to preserve our national veto in areas such as taxation and social security where it is right that member states

should have the final say over matters that affect their vital national interests.

All of the above measures bring the goal of EU enlargement to Eastern and Southern Europe one step closer. This has huge implications for us all. The government has been a consistent champion of the enlargement process. Whether one looks at this from a local, national, or European perspective, the benefits of a wider EU are manifest.

Enlargement will enhance security and stability in Europe. The EU countries have been at peace for over 50 years. We now have the opportunity to extend security to former members of the Warsaw Pact, and thus make us all safer. Enlargement will bring down barriers to trade and business. Companies in the UK could benefit from a 40 per cent increase in the size of an enlarged single market, with more than 500 million consumers; and enlargement will benefit consumers, giving them access to a wider range of goods and services. It will also increase the opportunity for EU citizens to travel, live, and work in Central, Eastern, and Southern Europe. And finally enlargement will increase economic growth and prosperity. Independent research shows that the accession of the seven largest Central European applicants could boost Britain's GDP by £1.75 billion.

Given these overwhelming benefits, it is difficult to reconcile the reality of the Nice Treaty with the calls from some quarters to reject it and the wild claims of its detractors that it marks the latest staging post on the road to the European superstate. On the contrary, at Nice the EU's constituent parts, the member countries, demonstrated that the abiding truth of the Union is to bring sovereign nations together, giving them a common strength greater than any one of them could possess alone.

But our critics will continue to contend that the hidden agenda of most member states is to create a superstate which submerges our national identities. Nice demonstrated that this was emphatically not the case. But please don't take my word for it. Look at the recent statements of some of Europe's leading figures:

'Federalism is the model of the past.' (Giuliano Amato)

'A European superstate based in Brussels. This, frankly, is nonsense.' (Romano Prodi)

'Europe will never be a federation on the US model.' (Joschka Fisher)

'A United Europe of States, not a United States of Europe.' (Jacques Chirac)

But there is no greater testimony to the benefits we derive from EU membership than the desire of the applicants themselves to be part of the Union. There must be something good about a club which almost everyone wants to join. Reuniting Europe in the open, outward-looking EU we are shaping is a historic task. We owe it to the applicants—and our own peoples—to succeed.

HARMONIZATION OR FLEXIBILITY

William Hague

Earlier this year I spoke at the 20th conference of the European Democrat Union in Berlin. Assembled at that conference were leaders from Conservative, Christian Democrat, and other like-minded parties from across the European continent—European Democrats from Slovakia to Sweden, Cyprus to the Czech Republic. The gathering illustrated the historic challenge now facing Europe: the need finally to unite a great continent, divided for half a century by tyranny and dictatorship.

But why has this process taken so long? Why, more than ten years after the collapse of communism, are these countries still waiting patiently in line outside the EU's gates? These questions go to the heart of the debate about the choice now facing Europe. Enlargement of the EU has crystallized that choice as never before. Europe is now at a fork in the road. It will be choosing one of two routes.

On the one hand, it can carry on as it has. It can continue to drive relentlessly towards harmonization and integration. National interests will vary even more in an enlarged Europe of diverse nation-states. If they wish, Europe's leaders can continue to think that the only way to deal with this development is to be ever more ruthless in overriding those interests. They can continue to take more and more decisions in Brussels and fewer and fewer at the national level. They can continue down the route towards ever more majority voting, towards one currency, one tax policy, one employment policy, one defence policy, one legal area—in short, taking Europe towards what Tony Blair calls a superpower, but what is in effect a superstate, step by step. This is the route the EU has chosen so far. And it is precisely this which has delayed enlargement.

EU leaders have been trying to shoe-horn a continent of proud and independent nations, in all their glorious diversity, into rigid uniformity. They seem to think the EU has to be 'one size fits all'. The result has been a growing sense of alienation on the part of the peoples of Europe from their leaders and from the EU institutions.

None of this is inevitable. There is a better choice, an alternative vision for the future of the EU—one which recognizes that a diverse, enlarged Europe in a modern, fast-moving world has got to change. This would be an EU characterized by flexibility and reform. Under this vision, member states would have more room for manoeuvre. No longer would everyone have to adopt each and every new regulation and directive, no matter how burdensome and how inimical to their national interest. Each country would be able to get together with others in different combinations for different purposes and to a different extent — a 'network Europe' for a network world.

This general principle of greater flexibility in Europe is already gaining ground. Conservatives want to take it further. We have set out plans for a treaty flexibility provision so that, outside the areas of the single market and core elements of an open, free-trading, and competitive EU, countries need only participate in new legislative actions at a European level if they see this as in their national interest. Such flexibility would help to reconnect Europe with its citizens. It would address the problem of people's sense of alienation from EU institutions and their perceived helplessness when it comes to the direction in which the EU is heading. It would tackle the so-called 'democratic deficit' in Europe in the only real way in which it can adequately be tackled: by returning more decision-making power to the nation-state. Under a more flexible Europe, governments would be more accountable to their electorates for the choices they make.

Our proposals would reduce the constant tension between those countries which feel the process of integration is going too slowly and that others are holding them back, and those countries which feel they are being dragged against their will into a superstate. In short, a diverse and flexible Europe would be a Europe in touch with its people. And it would make the British people more willing partners in the EU enterprise. It would make a reality of Britain being in Europe, not run by Europe.

There are many specific areas in which reform is required to turn such a Europe into practice. A priority has to be the Common Agricultural Policy. In its current state, the CAP represents the single biggest impediment to speedy enlargement—and to the EU getting its budget under control for the sake of Europe's taxpayers. Today's CAP is indefensible socially, economically, ecologically, environmentally, and morally. It needs drastic change.

We believe that there should be greater national responsibility, where decisions currently taken at EU level would be better taken by the governments of individual member states. Prior to the Nice summit in December, the Conservative Party put forward a package of positive proposals that would have encouraged the creation of just such an outward-looking, enlarged, reformed EU. It was Europe's failure to move in this direction that made Nice such a tragically wasted opportunity. Instead, the summit resulted in a treaty that would take Europe down the road of ever greater integration. Its effect would be to reduce significantly the ability of British governments to block future EU measures which are not in the interests of the British people. This is precisely the wrong approach.

So we have made it clear that a Conservative government would not ratify the Treaty as it stands. Far from the current Treaty being helpful to the process of EU enlargement, as the Government claims, it is precisely such a pursuit of uniform integration that has already delayed enlargement. An integrationist Treaty would make successful enlargement less likely in the future. Of course, the

Conservative Party is strongly supportive of those measures discussed at Nice that genuinely concern enlargement—such as the reform of the Commission and the reweighting of votes in the European Council. We could agree tomorrow to ratify a Treaty that contained such measures. But what we cannot and will not endorse are measures of closer integration.

This, then, is the choice now facing Europe. I believe that the Conservative vision is right not just for Britain but for Europe as a whole. It would mean a Europe of cooperating sovereign states; a flexible Europe; an outward-looking and dynamic Europe; and a Europe that embraces the whole of our continent. It needs British leadership to start putting the case for this kind of Europe. But instead, the present government merely 'goes with the flow', adopting an integrationist agenda set by other EU leaders.

On the one hand we have a Labour Party which is actually busy taking us step by step to a superstate. It is a party which would ratify the Nice Treaty as it stands, and which is prepared to go even further towards a superstate in another summit now planned for 2004. It is a party which supports the so-called 'Charter of Fundamental Rights', a job-destroying charter for interference in national law. It is a party which has signed up to a European army, outside NATO, which clearly risks undermining NATO. And it is a party committed to scrapping our national currency—and with it our ability to set our interest rates to suit our needs—as soon as they think they can get away with it.

But Britain has another choice. It can choose a Conservative Party which will work to halt the one-way slide to a superstate; a party which will keep the pound; a party which will ensure that the Nice Treaty meets the requirements of the twenty-first century.

AN END TO VACILLATION
Charles Kennedy

The whole of Britain's post-war political history has been dominated by the question of Britain's relationship with Europe, as successive governments have continued to vacillate and procrastinate over Britain's relations with its continental neighbours. Now, in the age of globalization, the European debate must be conducted in a more positive form. Only by being constructively engaged in Europe can Britain have a real influence on the shape of the EU. Unless we are willing members, we will end up dealing with the consequences of decisions that affect us, but upon which we have not had sufficient influence.

Yet we have much to gain from Europe and membership of the euro. It is in Britain's long-term interests to join. So I am always amazed when the suggestion is made that engaging in Europe somehow involves selling-out on our interests — with the implication that pro-Europeans are unpatriotic. The reality is that to fully engage in Europe would be a patriotic move for Britain because it would promote our interests and allow us to exert a real influence.

The anti-European case is not at all credible. The sceptics try to argue that they are not anti-European, only anti-euro. In fact the two amount to much the same thing because, by and large, the anti-euro case is imbued with paranoid fears of domination from the continent, and a belief that, by joining the euro, we would end hundreds of years of proud independence. But the idea of Britain achieving anything in 'splendid isolation' is profoundly outdated.

The EU takes 55 per cent of our exports. The euro will be a major player in the global financial markets and it will become invaluable in securing the economic stability that many British industries are crying out for. When the exchange rate is right for British entry (a decision that the Liberal Democrats believe should be made by an independent commission of experts from business, financial, academic, and political backgrounds), membership of the euro will clearly be in Britain's business interest. Anything that can be done to open up European markets further to British business can only help.

But if we stay out of the euro, many British businesses will have to make the transition themselves, in order to trade and compete with companies in the eurozone. And they will suffer far more if they do not have the backing of the government. One of Gordon Brown's 'five tests' of wisdom for joining the euro is whether monetary union will encourage long-term investment in British business. While we cannot be sure that it will, we can be certain that being outside will discourage inward investment. If we hang back from joining the euro, foreign investors will start to hang back from Britain.

However, politicians will be failing the people if they continue to discuss Europe solely in the context of the single currency—and this is just what they are doing at the moment. There are also many other issues just as important, where European cooperation is vital and where the EU can deliver benefits for all people.

It can offer the chance for regions to become the most important level of government after the EU, with far fewer decisions taken in a national context that are completely irrelevant and ineffective when applied at regional level. In Britain we are now in an era of post-devolution politics, but there is still a great deal that needs to be done to give people more control over government. It is difficult to envisage a British future without English regional assemblies. Increasingly, English regions are looking to Scotland, Wales, Northern Ireland, and the continent and seeing how they are losing out. If you are a teacher in England, and you see that in one week teachers in Scotland are given a 20 per cent pay rise, and in Northern Ireland bureaucratic school league tables are abolished, you must start wondering whether a bit more power for England would be a good idea.

Meanwhile, regions across Europe with their own governments are becoming adept at competing to attract inward investment. The English regions need support to be given the chance to compete on equal terms. The challenge is to build a truly civic Britain, where power has been devolved to the local and regional level, and where we are playing a full part in Europe. Europe can spread power to the people. It is this regional framework in Europe that can help promote and strengthen diversity and empower people.

But as an enthusiastic advocate of Europe, I also recognize that if Europe is to be truly representative there will be an equally important need for reform. The duties and the sphere of influence of the European Parliament must be clearly defined alongside the duties and sphere of influence of national governments. Europe would have the power to act decisively with the agreement of all and, just as importantly, Europe would be kept out of areas in which it has no business. The European Parliament also needs to be given greater powers of scrutiny over the European Commission. It cannot be right that the elected body, the Parliament, does not have more control of the unelected institutions.

With the EU reformed, Europe can make a difference where only it can be effective. But if it is to have real authority in the global community then it will need to enlarge. Including Central and Eastern Europe within its boundaries will make the EU both more effective and more stable. That will help us all: if enlargement spreads security, prosperity, and democracy across Central and Eastern Europe, our own security and prosperity will be increased.

Action on a global scale has to be the ultimate goal, but in striving for worldwide solutions, cooperation between neighbours is the only way forward. A key starting point is to create a core bloc of countries who together have the power and influence to make a difference. Europe can be such a bloc, but only if today's politicians have the sense to put forward the arguments and have the courage to make it a reality. Europe can provide a strong voice for Britain throughout the world.

We must take the pro-European case to the country whenever we can, in order to prove some of the basic arguments, and debate with the eurosceptics to highlight the weakness of their case. I believe that the nation will eventually support those who want Britain to play a part in Europe. Britain's distinctive history and character, and the strength of its traditions, mean that our country has nothing to fear from involvement in the EU. We are strong enough to resist being swamped and strong enough to make a real difference. Far from meaning that it is not necessary for us to be part of the EU, our uniqueness makes it all the more possible to benefit from it.

APPENDIX 1: THE FIVE ECONOMIC TESTS

The chancellor of the exchequer, Gordon Brown, set out in July 1997 the five tests which he said he would use to assess whether it was in the national economic interest to join the single currency. Since then they have sometimes been phrased in slightly varying ways, and they are often summarized as 'investment, financial services, convergence, flexibility, and jobs'. The initial formulation was as follows:

- First: would joining EMU create better conditions for firms making long-term decisions to invest in Britain?
- Second: how would adopting the new currency affect our financial services?
- Third: even if there are long-term benefits from EMU, are business cycles and economic structures compatible so that we and others in Europe could live comfortably with euro interest rates on a permanent basis?
- Fourth: if problems do emerge, is there sufficient flexibility to deal with them?
- Fifth, the bottom line: will joining EMU help to promote higher growth, stability, and a lasting increase in jobs?

APPENDIX 2: MEMBER AND CANDIDATE STATES

Member states

The EU's member states (with year of joining) are:

Austria* (1995)
Belgium* (1958, founding member)
Denmark (1973)
Finland* (1995)
France* (1958, founding member)
Germany* (1958, founding member)
Greece* (1982)
Ireland* (1973)
Italy* (1958, founding member)
Luxembourg* (1958, founding member)
Netherlands* (1958, founding member)
Portugal* (1986)
Spain* (1986)
Sweden (1995)
United Kingdom (1973)

*The country belongs to the single currency group.

Candidate states

Negotiations on terms for accession have started with all
of the following countries with the exception of Turkey:

Bulgaria
Cyprus
Czech Republic
Estonia
Hungary
Latvia
Lithuania
Malta
Poland
Romania
Slovakia
Slovenia
Turkey

CHRONOLOGY

July 1952	Six countries form the European Coal and Steel Community.
March 1957	The ECSC countries sign the Treaty of Rome, which creates the European Economic Community and Euratom.
January 1958	The EEC and Euratom come into being.
August 1961	The UK applies to join the EEC.
January 1962	The Common Agricultural Policy is created.
January 1963	De Gaulle vetoes UK membership.
May 1967	The UK again applies to join.
July 1967	Merger of EEC, European Steel and Coal Community, and Euratom into the European Community.
December 1967	De Gaulle again vetoes UK membership.
January 1973	The UK joins the EC.

1974/5   Labour government 'renegotiates' the conditions of entry.

June 1975   Referendum in which the UK votes to stay in.

March 1979   Exchange Rate Mechanism comes into operation.

June 1979   First direct elections to the European Parliament.

June 1984   Fontainebleau summit agrees rebate on Britain's budget contribution.

February 1986   Single European Act signed in Luxembourg.

October 1990   The UK joins the Exchange Rate Mechanism.

December 1991   Maastricht summit (Treaty signed in February 1992).

June 1992   Danish referendum rejects Maastricht Treaty.

September 1992 The UK is forced out of the Exchange Rate Mechanism.

1992   Single market programme largely completed.

May 1993   Second Danish referendum endorses Maastricht Treaty.

CHRONOLOGY

November 1993   Maastricht Treaty comes into force, creating the European Union.

March 1995   Schengen Agreement on open borders comes into force.

June 1997   Amsterdam Treaty agreed; the UK accepts the Social Chapter.

January 1999   Economic and monetary union begins for 11 countries.

March 1999   Entire Commission resigns over claims of fraud and mismanagement.

GLOSSARY

Agenda 2000	Commission proposals to reform the CAP and other policies ahead of enlargement
CAP	Common Agricultural Policy
CFP	Common Fisheries Policy
CFSP	Common Foreign and Security Policy
Committee of the Regions	Advisory committee with representatives of local authorities
Council of Ministers	Composed of ministerial representatives from each member state, the final decision-making body of the EU
Ecofin	Meeting of EU economics and finance ministers
Economic and Social Committee	Advisory committee including unions, employers, and other sectional interests
ECSC	European Coal and Steel Community, formed in 1952; precursor to the EEC, it placed coal and steel production in six countries under a single authority

EEC	European Economic Community
EMU	Economic and Monetary Union, process ending in the replacement of national currencies by a single currency
enhanced cooperation	Process allowing states who want to proceed further with integration in certain areas to do so (also called 'reinforced cooperation')
ESDP	European Security and Defence Policy
ERM	Exchange Rate Mechanism
Euratom	European Atomic Energy Community, established in 1958 to promote cooperation in the use of atomic energy
Euro-12	Group of finance ministers of states who are in the single currency
European Commission	Formed of two Commissioners from each of the larger countries and one each from the smaller ones, this initiates and implements EU legislation
European Council	Meeting of EU heads of government, at least once in each six-month presidency (official term for 'summit')
European Parliament	Directly elected since 1979, it has garnered gradually increasing powers over legislation and the Commission

European Union Created by the Maastricht Treaty, which came into force in 1993

eurozone Those states in the single currency

GATT Predecessor to the WTO

Inter-Governmental Conference Long-running series of meetings to revise the EU's Treaty (the next one is set for 2004)

NAFTA North American Free Trade Area; it comprises the US, Canada, and Mexico

pillar Under the Maastricht Treaty the EU's work is divided into three 'pillars'. The first consists of the traditional areas of activity that were already pursued by the European Community (trade, agri-culture, environment, employment, etc.). The Treaty added two new pillars to this—the Common Foreign and Security Policy and cooperation on justice and home affairs.

presidency The right to chair meetings of the Council of Ministers and European Council; rotates through all member states on a six-monthly basis

qualified majority voting Procedure for voting within the Council of Ministers in which each country's votes are weighted by population, and measures require a certain proportion of votes to pass. Currently a qualified majority will require 62 votes out of 87 (the UK has 10); this will change under enlargement.

Schengen Agreement — Allows open borders between participating countries (not the UK or Ireland)

Single European Act — Reform of the Treaty of Rome, signed in 1986, which among other things paved the way for the single market

subsidiarity — Principle that action should only be taken at a European level when it would be more effective than taking action at a national level

Treaty of Rome — Signed in 1957, founding document for the EEC

WTO — World Trade Organization, successor to GATT; regulates international trade with the aim of reducing barriers